M000121563

How I sold a million copies of my software . . .

▶ and how you can, too!

How I sold a million copies of my software . . .

▶ and how you can, too!

Herbert R. Kraft

Adams Media Corporation

HOLBROOK, MASSACHUSETTS

To my namesake Herbert K. Frie

ACKNOWLEDGMENTS: Although all errors are mine, many persons over the years may see what they told me, or at least what I thought I heard, in print. Thanks to (in no particular order): Warren Clary, Ray Clary, David Byron, George Johnson, Phil Sego, Paul Mayer, Jim Button, Members of the ASP, ASAD and DPA, Leonard Reed, Randy Jick, Ray Allen, Jeff Fryer, Chris Marinacci, Ron Paludan, and Ray Hogue.

Copyright ©1997, Herbert R. Kraft. All rights reserved.
This book, or parts thereof, may not be reproduced in any form without permission from the publisher; exceptions are made for brief excerpts used in published reviews.

Published by Adams Media Corporation
260 Center Street, Holbrook, MA 02343

ISBN: 1-55850-724-8

Printed in the United States of America.

J I H G F E D C B A

Library of Congress Cataloging-in-Publication Data
Kraft, Herbert R.
How I sold a million copies of my software / by Herbert R. Kraft.
— 1st ed.
Includes bibliographical references and index.
ISBN 1-55850-724-8
1. Computer software — Marketing. 2. Selling — Computer programs.
I. Title.
HF5439.C67K7   1997
005.3'068'8 — dc21   97-8836
CIP

This publication is designed to provide accurate and authoritative information with regard to the subject matter covered. It is sold with the understanding that the publisher is not engaged in rendering legal, accounting, or other professional advice. If legal advice or other expert assistance is required, the services of a competent professional person should be sought.
— From a *Declaration of Principles* jointly adopted by a Committee of the American Bar Association and a Committee of Publishers and Associations

Copyright is not claimed as to U.S. government works appearing in Appendices 2 (Library of Congress mission statement) and 3 (Federal Acquisition Regulations Extract).

This book is available at quantity discounts for bulk purchases.
For information, call 1-800-872-5627 (in Massachusetts, call 617-767-8100).

Visit our home page at http://www.adamsmedia.com

▷ Table of Contents

IV. Appendixes

CHAPTER 1

▷ Introduction

I'm honored that you've chosen to read *How I Sold a Million Copies of My Software*. You've set a lofty goal, and with commitment and passion, and the aid of this book, you too will be able to sell a million units.

Perhaps you are wondering what qualifies me to write this book. Other than the fact that I deal with industry insiders every day, I have a series of unique qualifications for writing about mass market software. To develop mass market software, you must have skills in programming, marketing, management, public relations, and law, besides having industry-specific knowledge.

I have acted as the "executive producer" of a series of computer programs that have, with minor changes, reached well over two million units in distribution, and they continue to sell at an increasing pace. The legal document and legal information series that I spearheaded wasn't an overnight success; I failed at the beginning, as you may.

I was fortunate to participate in one of the first college-level programs designed to encourage entrepreneurship at New College, Sarasota, Florida, in 1978. One of the lasting lessons of the program was that it takes almost every successful entrepreneur several iterations of financing, development, hard knocks, and starting over before winning at the game.

After graduating from law school, I practiced law only to discover that the legal field was overcrowded and overstressed. To "escape" from an unhappy career, I spent most of my available time learning computer skills and then assembling a team to develop a mass market legal self-help software series. Along the way, I met Jim Button and Paul Mayer, then on the board of the Association of Shareware

Professionals. They convinced me to look at shareware and low-cost retail as one of the markets for my software. This resulted in a shareware program that placed second and third in independent distribution ratings of shareware programs in 1990 and 1991. I've also donated extensive time to shareware and software organizations as a legal advisor.

In another happy accident, I financed my education by working in radio as both talent and management. I also hosted two nationally syndicated radio series on computer software in the mid-1990s. This provided a background in marketing and retailing that has come in very handy. Because the radio business depends so heavily on retail advertising, you must learn a great deal about marketing and promotion at the retail level to be a success in the industry.

I applied this unique background to become director of publishing for Cosmi, a software powerhouse that is experiencing sales growth well above that of its competitors. Independent software sales tracking organizations place Cosmi in the top twenty largest publishers in the United States, in terms of units sold. At Cosmi, I was in the "nerve center" of activity in the software industry, dealing with all the major retailers, distributors, agents, tool vendors, and independent developers.

Reading *How I Sold a Million Copies of My Software* is an investment in your education that will pay huge dividends. Whether you agree or disagree with my observations, this book contains a huge amount of "food for thought."

With the perspective that you'll acquire by reading this book, you'll be far ahead in the game. To make this book more valuable, I've arranged the "Your Big Break" contest, where the author of what we judge to be the best program for commercial sale will receive a publishing agreement for mass market distribution (see Chapter 11).

This book is not an autobiography, nor is it another one of the never-ending stream of corporate apologies by computer industry mavens justifying their existence. You should take the time to read books by the founders of large software companies to learn what made them successful. To make the record clear, although it's possible to franchise hot dog stands or hair cutting salons, and although there are some good practices and some poor ones that I can warn you about, there is no one solution, no one formula, to make a million-seller. On the other hand, *How I Sold a Million* will make your pathway to success shorter by showing you how to avoid many mistakes — particularly when first designing your program's concepts and distribution.

I have consciously avoided coloring what I have to say in these chapters solely by my experience. This isn't to say that I don't have biases. Please allow me a brief period of grandstanding; I owe it to you to reveal the formula that I, along with the rest of the team who toiled long and hard, used to make the million-selling program a reality.

First and foremost, give and give and give and then give some more. Although a title whose features and value for the price put it in the middle of the pack can sell a million units, make it easier on yourself. Produce a product that compares favorably with $99 titles, then sell it at $19 or even $9, and then give some more until it really hurts. The computer software consumer is much wiser than you think. Instead of thinking that you never go wrong underestimating the intelligence of the consumer, you should assume that the customer knows what a good value is.

Since software sales are made on impulse, the simplest way to make it to a million sales is to make your program the best value possible. The more features (with their related benefits that you describe on the box), the lower your price, and the higher your quality, the better your sales. It's really that simple. Do it faster, cheaper, and better, but do it with as much energy and enthusiasm as you can. Energy and enthusiasm are the keys to success. Good luck — and get to work!

Herb Kraft
Hermosa Beach, California
January 1997

PART I

▷ Design and Packaging

CHAPTER 2

▷ Successful Topics for Mass Markets

With millions of computers in use worldwide, the odds are that almost any topic that can be treated as a computer program has a million potential users at some price point. However, even having sold a million units, the program can still be a financial failure. That can happen under several different scenarios.

The first case is a program that is so expensive to launch that you cannot amortize the product over mass market sales volumes. An operating system that is totally compatible with the existing dominant system might sell multiple million units if it were priced at $15 per copy for an original equipment manufacturer (OEM) license. (At the time that this chapter is being written, this would provide an approximate 75 percent discount from the OEM license for the dominant operating systems.)

The market is likely to be OEM since users are unlikely to drop their current operating system and pay for a new one. Users normally acquire their operating systems bundled with their computers. Second, OEMs are unlikely to support a new operating system, even one that is totally compatible with present standards, unless the price difference was so much that they would see an immediate profit and have enough cushion to handle advertising and promoting the system.

Even though your order book for this hypothetical operating system would probably be full, the total financial commitment to produce an operating system and then market it would probably dwarf the financial returns from sales.

Of course, you could not afford to assume that the large and well-capitalized companies that provide operating systems would not effectively retaliate on price. Catastrophic losses are certain if the other operating system vendors match or beat your price. Business-school texts are full of case studies of failure by a new entrant to gain market share in a product niche by low price alone. This has happened with pain killers, cereals, and airline passenger fares.

Every rule has its exceptions. In a market that has many players and low margins, a low-cost competitor can ultimately reduce the consumer's threshold for software prices. However, this is a long-term strategy and requires significant capitalization and staying power.

Another failure scenario would be a program that had horrible sell through at each outlet, but you were able to continue to locate outlets. Although this, too, would result in a million copies sold, slotting fees and returns would destroy the company while it persisted in locating new venues for poor programs.

Therefore, you must not only design for mass market sales, but for profitable mass market sales. As noted in Chapter 10, retailers systematically remove any program from their shelves that does not sell through (the rate at which product shipped to retailers sells to end users). So we must refine our quest for a scenario in which we could sell a million net programs profitably.

The most profitable programs are the "slow best-sellers." These are programs that rarely hit "the top of the charts," but consistently move and have long shelf lives. Drawing a comparison to the field of book publishing, some titles like hot novels sell many copies very quickly and then fizzle out — normally with high returns. The return levels are high because by the time the publisher sees large numbers and then commits to more press runs, the interest in the book is dwindling. The publisher sells a million copies but has to pulp another million. The net result of the million sales and million returns is zero sales. You can't pulp disks, CDs, or packaging, so a product once completed is probably going to be sold as is or destroyed.

Compare a program that hits the top of the best-seller charts to a title that has a four- or five-year shelf life and sells ten thousand to forty thousand units monthly. The odds are that there will be few if any returns of a program that sells consistently for years, and although the payouts to the author and publisher are slower, the net result is a higher cash present value to the author.

Software that can sell a million copies must be mass market, rather than vertical market, software. To succeed, you must understand the difference between a large market and a mass market. There is no more critical concept in this field. Most programs designed for retail fail because the developer selected a large market rather than a mass market. Any market with more than 25 million potential users is a mass market.

In order to reach a million sales, your program will have to sell to approximately 2 to 3 percent of the computer users in North America, which is by far the largest market for software in the world, and make sales in at least a few overseas markets. This is an extremely daunting task, so you should do anything you can to broaden the potential market.

You cannot assume that you will reach a much higher percentage of a smaller market. Other than operating system software, few applications have penetrated more than 10 percent of the available market. Thus, if your target is 2 million users, reaching a million sales is probably impossible, even with unlimited resources. The highest market penetration of software other than operating systems is about 40 percent, which dominant word processors have reached from time to time.

Software for legal professionals, for instance, is a large but vertical market, perhaps as many as 2 million persons if you count paralegals, law students, and persons in legal-related businesses such as banking or real estate. However, persons who have legal concerns is a mass market — it is as large as the entire computer marketplace. Many well-intentioned persons suggested that I concentrate on sales to lawyers. That advice was clearly wrong. Although many lawyers and paralegals buy legal programs, the "persons with legal concerns" market dwarfs the professional, legal market.

However, in casting your program as a mass market one, the difference is one of focus and packaging rather than content. It may be necessary to provide two levels of menus or to put "advanced" features in drop-down menus, which is good programming practice anyway. Here are some examples.

Tax form preparation: large market — accountants, CPAs, and tax preparers; mass market — people who need to file tax forms

Reading skills: large market — elementary school teachers; mass market — people who care about children (that includes parents, uncles, aunts, older siblings, and grandparents)

Virus detection: large market — computer technicians; mass market — people who are concerned about viruses

Only a handful of scientific studies have been made concerning the demographics of the typical purchaser of computer software at retail. The statistics are extremely humbling. Eighty-five percent of all sales are made on impulse. Only about one in ten of the sales that you will ever make was because the customer discerned a need for your software. Consider this humbling fact when planning your program.

The consensus among insiders is that the typical purchaser of retail software is a thirty- to forty-year-old male with some college education, who is purchasing the software for his own use. This information concerning typical purchasers should be used in design although efforts need to be made to reach other purchasers.

Although I can provide general guidelines for topics that have the best chance to make it as mass market software, picking topics for hit computer software programs is a subjective skill, and a gift. Even the best publishing and marketing teams can only hope to have a very high ratio of hits to bombs.

One of the most important skills to learn is not to design programs for yourself or peer group. You must design a program for mass market sales to fit the desires of a significant part of the computer-buying public. Unfortunately, compared to a million or more computer users, programmers and professionals in the computer field have very different views of what would be a useful program. In a software organization, those who are the most likely to know are the sales staff. They are "close to the ground" and have real-world knowledge about the truth that's in the trenches.

If you are passionate about a topic, nothing that I can write will dissuade you from releasing the program. However, swimming with the current is easier than traveling upstream, and the guidelines that I provide will maximize the chance of a commercially successful release.

TITLES WITH THE LEAST CHANCE OF SUCCESS

This book is a blueprint for developing software with the greatest chance of success. The industry "legend" suggests that certain types of titles have characteristically been poor choices. Someone is working right now to prove industry knowledge wrong, but these industry legends are the result of a great deal of experience and probably reflect structural imperatives in the computer marketplace.

You should also note that many of these categories are still excellent for "large market" sales but don't make the grade for mass market sales. However, most of the fields that I suggest that you avoid generally not only fail to produce mass market program success, they also fail to be profitable at all. If you are willing to be satisfied with less than a million sales so long as you make a profit, these areas are still bad bets.

GAMES

Games are excellent sales performers if measured as a category in total. Measured individually, the story is bleak. The chance of any individual game succeeding is slim. Research shows that the top twenty or so games can gobble up 90 percent of revenue. In other words, unless a game is one of a few big hits, the odds are that it will not succeed financially. The other difficulty is that the acceptance of games is freakish. An editorial team at a general publisher can often guess with 80 percent or more success the probable sales of a title. (Another question is whether this is a self-fulfilling prophecy.) It is almost impossible to make sensible guesses on games.

Games tend to be a bad gamble for an entirely different set of reasons. One is that games now have the highest development costs. In the most recent years, games have started to feature named actors as performers, and dollar figures sound like the budgets for major motion pictures. Many games now being released are touted in trade magazines as being launched with $2 or $3 million initial advertising budgets.

Bringing a new title to market is usually a minimum commitment of $100,000 to $250,000. Games tend to cost $2 million or more because of the intensive nature of graphics and technology needed, together with the fact that games have dozens of levels, requiring huge amounts of coding. Add to that the millions of dollars spent just in opening advertising, and you begin to realize that the money would be better used in making eight or ten more titles than in "betting the farm" on one game concept to be sold to the masses.

The concept that games are poor bets for mass market publishers is reinforced by the recent public statements by Martin Alper, the President and Chief Executive Officer of Virgin Interactive. Alper stated that the core market for games is about a million persons. Although large, it is *not* a mass market. In order to get to a million sales, you'd need 100 percent of the core market — an impossible level of penetration. Despite this estimation of the core market, Alper's best-seller in North America in 1996 reached only 500,000 units. This is clearly a great accomplishment, and a profitable one. But it is somewhat short of the mass market model.

Another indication of the status of the game market is from Gail Williams of Corel's CD-Home division. Williams feels that the supply of games "exceeds the demand." She concurs with Alper's view that publishers will release fewer and fewer games. Both of these insiders think that the game business will continue to be "hit driven" with the top games making almost all the money.

Perhaps the most telling reason that games are not a good bet is that even though there is virtually no software for it, "next generation" game machines from Nintendo and others sold out over the 1996 Christmas season, with buyers standing in line to make deposits on units yet to be made. There is a six- or seven-to-one price advantage in favor of dedicated video game systems compared to entry-level computers. Games should continue to be a soft market for personal computers.

Designing games is fun and, if your game is one of a handful of hits, profitable. Nevertheless, there is such a tide of negatives that it is not a good bet for the next several years.

MULTIMEDIA TRAVELOGUES

A number of multimedia travelogues have been released, and the output of them seems to be unabated by the fact that they do not sell. Computer software is unusually good at creating multimedia travel software, and the subject is a very rich one. The problem is probably packaging the titles singly and pricing the titles significantly too high. Nevertheless, there are whispers and knowing winks at trade shows when persons display these titles. If you listen, you can hear the whispering about "how bad everyone feels" for them. The larger question is whether the public wants to "travel" on their computer. Videotapes have better resolution, and web pages contain more up-to-date information than prepackaged programs.

WORD PROCESSORS

Word processors are characteristic of a number of applications that the new developer will probably not succeed in releasing for mass market use although they may do very well in a much smaller market. Word processing is a field in which applications such as Microsoft Word and Corel WordPerfect dominate the market. Even more so than in the case of games, all the market dollars are concentrated in a mere handful of applications.

If your only skills or interests are related to word processing, look at an add-on to the dominant programs as the best shot at hitting a million sales — and getting bought out by one of the owners of the dominant systems. Consider the story of companies like Central Point, which built empires on add-ons to operating systems, like "undelete" programs. On the other hand, the number of DOS shells and word processors that were marketed and flopped is huge. This is another area that insiders wince at when they see new programs introduced. Try your hand elsewhere.

BOOKS ON DISK

The traditional paper book is a tremendously efficient system for storing and retrieving information. Unlike computers, it is truly portable and the only "peripherals" needed are artificial illumination at night and a bookmark although in an emergency a page can be dog-eared. Computers should have a tremendous advantage over books since a single CD-ROM can hold more than 600 megabytes of data. Using data compression, a CD can hold more than 2 billion megabytes (2 gigabytes) of data, or roughly 5 million typed pages. Since a CD can be replicated for 40 to 50 cents at present market prices, on a storage basis, the computer is tremendously more cost effective.

Computers have an additional advantage. Video, images, and audio can accompany the presentation. On a theoretical basis, the advantage is to the computer. However, it all breaks down when you consider that the book doesn't need a computer to work. A book's portability makes it far superior to computers. Consider also that the user needs only to know how to read and doesn't need to know about computers: the learning curve is much lower for a book. Despite the computer revolution, the paper book industry has done very well, and I think will be around for a long time, experiencing significant growth. Do your part and buy an extra copy of this book.

Despite all the advantages that electronic books have over paper books, books on disks have generally been a failure and don't represent a good investment for developers.

CHILDREN'S SOFTWARE

Like games, children's software depends on advertising that must fire the rather fickle imaginations of kids. This is as much of a crap shoot as trying to sell trendy clothing to teenage girls. A few programs have broken through and become successes, like Where in the World is Carmen San Diego? However, almost every other entrant into the field has not only failed to make mass market sales, it has failed to be profitable.

PROGRAMMING TOOLS

Borland, Microsoft, IBM, and a few other players are locked in a "life or death" struggle for domination of programming tools. However, those at the top of the business sell millions of units. As a result, tools for relatively new languages are often given away to try to attract users. The programming tool marketplace has matured to the extent that in most cases companies are primarily selling upgrades of their programs to existing users, or competitive upgrades to their competitor's users. Because Microsoft and Borland have already made a great deal of revenue from selling $499 or $299 development platforms, they can afford to continue the massive development costs of keeping compilers and rapid application development (RAD) software up to date with $99 or less for upgrades and competitive upgrades. Given that the costs of entry are so high for programming tools intended for mass market sale, new companies probably can't match the $99 competitive upgrade price of other programming titles and still make a profit.

SEASONAL TITLES

A few companies have done well with tax preparation programs. However, any title that is seasonal is a headache for distribution. This requires that you obtain cooperation from retailers in precisely timing the release of the program. There are frequent glitches in distribution of software, and anything less than perfect distribution will result in a substantial dollar loss.

OFFICE SUITES

To be a success, an office suite must offer multiple interrelated applications — usually word processing, spreadsheet, database (mailing list), e-mail, and desktop publishing — and it must offer them in an interchangeable format. However, the advantage of interrelatedness is lost unless the program is virtually a standard. Bill Gates called the competitive advantage that accrues to a program that gets adopted as a standard, "a positive feedback cycle." Unless you can reach critical mass with an office suite, there is little point in entering the market.

TELEVISION AND MOVIE TIE-INS

Numerous computer programs feature clips from television programs and related material. These programs generally don't do well in sales because they do not constitute as strong a tie-in as their developers imagine.

TOPICS THAT DO NOT TRANSLATE WELL TO COMPUTERS

Computers excel at various tasks. However, there are many topics in which television, printed matter, or live presentations do better and are more accepted. For example, a collection of classical music with historical text and analysis is a poor choice of title because the audio resolution of computer speakers is worse than that of conventional stereo units. In creating a computer program, be sure that a computer is an efficient way to handle the task. If there is no compelling reason that a computer should do the task, pass. For example, no "grocery list" program has ever done well. It's hard to carry a computer with you when you look through your freezer to see what you need to buy. This area probably describes most failures in the marketplace.

SCREEN SAVERS

There are so many "free" screen savers and new types of screen savers, like Internet tickers, that the odds of breaking through in this market are very poor. If you must choose a battle to fight, one in which numerous competitors are giving away the product is not the one to pick.

TITLES WITH THE HIGHEST CHANCE OF SUCCESS

The following classes of titles are among the least glamorous, but day in and day out, slow-boil million-sellers are being created in these categories.

Single-purpose applications

After spending a career developing relatively complex software subject to "feature escalation," I am now becoming aware that mass market purchasers generally find computers too complicated. They show a preference, verifiable by sales reports, for single-purpose applications that do one thing very well. This is demonstrated by the huge sales of programs that do only one discrete task. Combine a strong feature list with a good concept and price point, and you have an excellent chance for sales success.

Small office, home office

Large corporations and governments are laying people off in what they term euphemistically as downsizing. The largest growth in employment is in small business. The persons who are making a go of small businesses are desperately short of time. Reasonably priced programs that fit their needs will sell very well.

Internet agents

Internet tickers and intelligent agents are "smart browsers," and the next step in telecommunications technology. Computers excel at interactive gathering of news. The battle in this market will be fierce, but the winners will build multiple empires on the strength of their agents.

THE GREATEST CHALLENGES WITH THE HIGHEST POSSIBLE RETURNS

I'd like to share a "wish list" of applications that would broaden the computer market. One of the biggest challenges that the computer industry faces is that penetration of computer users remains about the same. The areas that I am identifying would create further interest in computing. These programs may never be made or published, but if someone could reach the market that needs these applications, I am certain that multimillion unit sales would be in the offing.

The women's killer app

A challenge with a multimillion-dollar payoff is a "killer application" (or "app") for women or girls. Personal observation and statistics prove that men significantly outnumber women as purchasers of consumer software. All editorial directors in the software industry want to find a strategy to broaden the basis of the market to bring in more women. Maybe what is really needed is that women have more free time so that they can spend time in front of the computer.

The business planning tool, next generation

One of the applications that started the PC revolution was the spreadsheet. Although there have been improvements in spreadsheet technology, today's spreadsheets are much the same as the original CP/M spreadsheet programs. A new business planning tool that will capture the imagination of the businesspersons who are not yet using computers is a major winner and could start the next Microsoft or Netscape.

The personal-size computer application

The technology exists to make usable computers that fit in the palm of your hand. However, no application has yet emerged to make a miniaturized computer a must-have. This application, should it ever exist, will probably not be communication related because cellular phones and pagers seem to be doing quite well.

Speech interface

IBM and other vendors have developed rudimentary speech interface. Create a program that allows persons to bark orders to a computer like Star Fleet personnel, and you have a winner. Here's a hint. The odds are that present hardware is not up to this task. However, when special-purpose computer chips that handle speech recognition become available, start coding.

If you have a topic, and have refined the concept to make sure that it is sufficiently broad based to be of interest to a mass market, you must then do market research to determine if there are precedents for your approach. Very few prerelease scientific surveys or "focus groups" are used in planning software releases. However, research services like PC Data provide surveys of actual retail sales at selected retailers. These services show the past sales figures of virtually every program on the market. We will discuss several different ways to get market research. You will want to prepare a final research report of as many competitive programs as possible, comparing features, price points, and media.

Computer publishers maintain a library of catalogs from as many sources as possible, including large distributors' wholesale catalogs, competitors' catalogs, and multititle consumer catalogs. With the emergence of the Internet, publishers' web sites provide a wealth of information. These libraries are also histories. What was released in the past is just as important as the latest catalog entries. It is a very useful study to chart the development of titles similar to yours. By seeing changes that your competitors have made to their titles, you may be able to avoid a sequence of feature changes that has already been tried.

Although not decisive, the fact that others have failed in the past at the same topic that you have is important information. Before releasing a program that has failed before, find out why the other party failed. Was it price, distribution, or features? Be sure to do something different.

Before releasing a title, the most valuable research that you can do is to spend time in as many large computer stores as possible. Buying any competing programs is vital research. Besides running the programs, see how your proposed title would do in a "battle of the box." What could you explain, simply, about your program that would convince the purchaser to buy your program rather than a competitor's? As we note, having a unique selling point is important in making a success of your program. In particular, as explained in Chapter 3, having a USP (unique selling point) allows you to define the battle on your terms.

Think like an extremely skeptical consumer. What simple, direct message, or "sound byte," on the package will convince a customer to invest his or her money in your program rather than another's? Whatever your competitive advantages, if you can't express them on your box in a few words, the odds are against being able to use that advantage in the marketplace. Recall that more than 85 percent of all sales are impulse sales, which are sales made at the point of sale.

Your best and only realistic chance to make the sale is by box copy. As the industry changes, more and more programs are being sold in jewel cases without an exterior box. This limits your ability to use box copy, which is your primary way to sell your program to the impulse market. This is the best argument for picking and focusing on a USP.

In creating a title, consider using a model different from that of your competitors'. Organizing your title goes back to the familiar theme of the USP. Although there are many different ways to organize computer software titles, over time I have seen six patterns repeated. Programs are usually organized in these six basic ways, all of which are closely related to the program's USP.

THE BIGGEST

Feature escalation is now the organizing theme of many software programs. Packaging and economic factors limited most programs to five or six floppy disks.

This limits programs to a maximum of 6 or 7 megabytes of compressed data. CD-ROMs suddenly gave programmers the capability of working with 650 megabytes. The first generation of CDs were more than developers could fill; most of the first wave of programs occupied only 100 megabytes of space. However, the increasing use of video and the graphics requirements of graphical user interface programs have now combined to make using a fully compressed CD-ROM justifiable from an engineering standpoint.

ONE OF A SERIES

A number of games have proved that a "serialized" organization of a title is a successful marketing strategy. A recent look at best-seller lists show that various "editions" of Print Shop all were ranked as being in the top ten of various categories of sales. Corel has released a series of different collections of images. This will prove to be a more common strategy over time.

MULTIPLE PROGRAMS ON ONE DISK

This is one of the most fertile new ideas. Although program "suites" have been sold for as long as microcomputers, CDs have made it possible to offer several related programs in full format. Before CDs, video help and two-thousand-page online manuals were impossible. With 650-megabyte CD-ROMs it is possible to put video help and large manuals for several programs on one disk.

THE EASIEST

A battle is being waged between applications for the title of the easiest in the category. There is a customer backlash against powerful applications that require steep learning curves. Several companies are vying for the title of having the easiest total line of applications. One drawback of taking this approach is that you limit your market to computer-phobics. It is possible to take the position that a program is powerful and appealing to all computer users, yet has a simple interface. Nevertheless, dumbing-down is a program organization technique with much validity.

THE MOST ADVANCED

Even though many users crave simplicity, others want high performance and are undaunted by going through menus to reach commands. In the same way that insisting your program is the easiest narrows its potential sales, insisting that it is the high-performance leader has the same effect on the other end.

VALUE LEADER

Low price is not a significant factor in the sales of computer programs. However, the concept of "value software," good software at a discount to other programs' prices, is one of the industry areas with the greatest present growth and future potential. This is the model that I always gravitate toward. The recent best-selling book *Underdog Marketing* probably describes it best. There are two schools of pricing. The first is "what's the most we can charge," and the second is "what's the most we can give to the customer and still make a profit." Aggressively featured and engineered programs that are sold at a lower price than competitors', and that represent a true "good buy" to customers, have a huge potential market. They tend to be consistently good sellers and reach six-or seven-digit sales levels without significant returns.

CHAPTER 3

▷ Mass Market Programming and Design Issues

There are dozens of books on managing software projects. These all deal with the mechanics of motivating an entire team to think and to produce great programs for use within that team's company. No book covers mass market software engineering. Although computer programs designed for use by limited audiences — for example, a program for pharmacy management, or a program specifically intended for the mass market, like a general-purpose spreadsheet — have many similarities, they also have significant differences that require a new programming world view.

The most important issue in which mass market software differs from any other type of development is in the time pressure to get a program to market. Software for the mass market must be completed within four to six months. Every hour beyond six months subjects a program to lost opportunities and market risks.

Unfortunately, a number of well-capitalized software startups have failed because their business plan allowed one year for development. The companies failed, and in some cases, their program never even made it to market because by the time that they had reached a near release point in development, their programming teams rightfully declared the program obsolete. Technology had leap-frogged their design assumptions. Being forced to throw away one version and faced with another year of no revenue, several companies were unable to ever complete their project.

There are several reasons that the development cycle is four to six months. Although longer cycles may be acceptable for corporate or government projects, the commercial programmer is "shooting at a moving target." Haste, combined with progress, must be the order of the day.

I am not prescribing shipping awfully buggy code; instead, I am advocating that, if you have a functional program, go ahead and release it. Then spend another two weeks or a month to code that snazzy extra feature, and make that update available by the Internet. With the emergence of the net, it's possible to release a program that is not 100 percent ready for prime time, and "make it up" to users by offering a free upgrade to the next version, or even two. Use FTP (file transfer protocol) to distribute "get passworded" or encrypted updates to your users with virtually no cost to you. To cover the "Internet challenged," you can offer disks for $3.95 or so, plus mailing and handling.

If your development cycle were a year or longer, you'd have to guess what operating system will be "fashionable" or in use by the majority of your customers. It's risky to assume that users will upgrade to new systems, and design your program to work on a system that hasn't been released yet. Will memory prices drop, resulting in users having more memory on board? Users with more memory demand more complicated features.

Many programming teams want to be the first to have a particular application for a new operating system. If you program for an operating system that you expect will be released in the future, you have introduced a new wildcard into the game. As the delay in the release of Windows 95 showed, you may be frozen out of the marketplace. Moreover, if a widely adopted new operating system is released, it's going to attract all the consumer dollars for itself.

You also are placing a bet by assuming that the public will accept the next operating system. A number of developers followed this logic in coding for Atari ST, OS/2, and other systems that never made it to mass market status. If you put your eggs in one basket, even if you watch the basket, you may make an investment in creating mass market software for a market that never even becomes large.

Nevertheless, being one of the first programs to use a new operating system can lead to making a hit program. To do so, sanity requires that you have a plan B. As discussed in Chapter 10 whatever plans you make, a program may not "click."

Even a simple question such as whether to plan for CD distribution, disk, or DVD (Digital Video Disk) is significant — and utterly unknowable. Place your bets now, the roulette wheel is about to be spun. Anyone who thinks that he or she can predict the market parameters a year from now should read a book like *Dvorak Predicts*. There is no better connected or more insightful person in the computer industry than John Dvorak. Nevertheless, his 1994 book of predictions proved to be spectacularly wrong in almost every major category.

In many cases, the problem is not deciding to develop for upcoming technology — it's sticking with the existing technology, which is the right choice. For example, both corporate America and consumer end users have not adopted Windows 95 as fast as they did Windows 3.1. Staying with 16 bit has been a very smart bet for many developers during the 1995 to 1996 period.

Fast development is the only hedge that you can have against technological change. For as long as it is possible to imagine, there will be improvements in computers and peripherals, including:

Increases in the speed of microprocessors

Increases in storage capacity

Improvement in display resolution and size

Operating systems will also change. The introduction of Windows 95 by Microsoft was one of the major events of the year, both as an advertising event, since reportedly hundreds of millions of dollars was spent on its introduction, and, since the press rightfully considered the introduction, as a news event.

Just as important to software developers is the introduction of new tools that change the possibilities of development. You can anticipate the regular release of new and improved programming tools. A short development cycle allows your programmers to always use the latest versions of tools, or to at least use those new features in programming tools that are real improvements.

The present technology for development tools allows very rapid development. No topic is more controversial among programmers than the choice of language and development tools. Some programmers swear by C++, others find C++ nonmaintainable. Most software publishing organizations follow the practical rule of allowing outside developers to code as they please, and making few limits on the choices made by in-house programmers. Programming is an art, and programmers always will be most productive using tools of their own choice.

The most vital activity that a programmer can do is think. Everything that you can do to encourage thought is good; anything that hinders the output of intellectual activity is bad. Forcing a developer to use one language or tool rather than another adds an unnecessary distraction. Good programs can be written in any language, and "poor" languages can nevertheless be used to make excellent programs.

Some organizations require the use of standard development tools to permit true "teaming" on projects and to create a corporate library of reusable functions. If you read professional magazines about programming, you may believe that coding small functions designed for reuse is a new technique. However, it is an old, well-known strategy. When WordPerfect Corporation was a powerhouse organization, it developed libraries of reusable functions, coded in assembly language for extreme speed, and developed programs by "weaving" together a deliverable tapestry, the final program.

The most recent innovation in computer programming is the rapid application development (RAD) environment, typified by Visual Basic and Delphi. Earlier RADs were able to produce only "cookie cutter" applications that looked alike. Now that user interfaces are standardized, RAD tools are practical for producing real-world applications of any kind. The original battles of programming languages are being replayed as Microsoft and Borland again vie for supremacy among RAD tools.

The differences between the Borland, Microsoft, and other products are quite small; all the integrated development environments are excellent. I presently give the nod to Borland's Delphi, which is a truly compiled environment. That means that Delphi creates machine code. Visual Basic creates p code, an intermediate type of computer code, which is then interpreted by run times. As a result, the code made with Visual Basic runs slower, even with extensive optimization, because two steps are required to run the Visual Basic code.

For what it's worth, the best and brightest are on public record for speeding up development by using RADs to make the user interface. Hewlett-Packard uses Delphi to create the front end for all of their software products, like printer drivers, and then codes the actual drivers in C++. If you are starting from scratch, consider adopting a single RAD environment. Encourage development of your own library of generic functions and components that can be reused in later projects.

Since at least three uncontrollable variables affect development, the best hedge is to keep the development cycle short enough that the development team can intelligently plan the specifications and do enough, if required, to ride the wave of any introductions.

For example, if the release of a new operating system is imminent and a short development cycle is planned, the developer can nevertheless make some concessions at the last moment and have a significant head start if retooling is required. During the transition from DOS to Windows, developers on longer cycles often had to throw away a great deal of code and delay introduction of the program. Those on shorter cycles were able to make minimally compliant Windows versions of their programs and go ahead with a DOS release at once. Developers on shorter cycles had many more options. If work had to be cashiered, it was a lesser amount.

One other discipline that a short development cycle forces is compromise in design goals. Every programmer whom I have worked with has stated to me at one time or another that time pressure is their greatest enemy. A program can always be improved. Every line of code, procedure, method, or algorithm can be optimized for speed, or the user functionality can be increased. However, the program *must* be shipped. "A program is never done — it just ships." You must make a serious and clear commitment to making an excellent product, but you cannot hold off release to achieve the ever-elusive goal of doing it better.

A great plan for making it to the top of mass market sales is to adopt a unique selling point or "high concept," one feature in which your program is irresistibly better than anything on the market. Then relentlessly program to deliver on the USP. The sales staff presenting computer software to wholesale buyers have a minute or so at the best, and sometimes less to describe a new program. It's like a test in which the only question is "Can you justify your existence?" followed by a two-sentence limit. Many USPs are out there, and to make it as a mass market program, you must design your program to have one. Although I talk about USPs in the singular, in communicating a USP, you can combine two concepts to create your niche.

Consider the USPs of several mass market successes:

- Duke Nukem — lots of gore *and* in 3-D

- Turbo Pascal — the world's fastest compiler at 350,000 lines a minute *and* at an affordable price

- PC Law Library series — ten times the legal forms as the other programs *and* at a lower price

- Peachtree accounting — more reports than any other accounting program *and* at a lower price

- Lotus 1-2-3 — business and accounting spreadsheet standard *and* supports third-party worksheets

Any superlative can be cast as a USP: faster, cheaper, bigger, heavier, lighter, simpler.

As the engineering manager of a mass market program, you must have a realistic approach to the design of your program and a relentless concentration on the USP. Computer programs *are* sold by the cover. If you have never done so, go to a large computer retailer and ask for permission to unobtrusively watch people actually buying programs. Customers look for clear points of differentiation between programs, generally price and features. (Pricing of programs is covered in Chapter 4.) You will observe that customers check for quantifiable USPs. Does an accounting program prepare 150 or 300 financial reports? Customers generally assume that the program with 300 reports is twice as good as the program with 150. This ignores the fact that most companies actually use only four or five of the reports, and the quality of these reports should be the real decision point. "Creeping featuritis" or "feature escalation" is a viable strategy to winning market share.

The focus on a USP is an effort to define the battle in your terms and then to focus the fight for consumer dollars on your terms. Place yourself in your customer's shoes and pick an issue that is easily explained on a box, and hit hard on that issue. Remember that after picking up the box, the customer will spend only twenty seconds looking at your program. Hit the customer hard with your best shot.

When planning your program, also bear in mind that features are relevant to your customers because of their benefits. You must reach an equilibrium in design and marketing in which you stress your program's features but ensure that your customer understands the benefits. For example, an accounting program with hundreds of reports leads to the benefit of the user being able to manage his or her business better and increase profit. A word processor that contains the capability to create web pages describes a feature. The benefit is that the user can put his or her business or hobbies on the Internet. A legal forms program with hundreds of documents is a feature. The benefit is that the user can protect his or her legal rights and take care of loved ones. In making a final decision to buy or not buy, the customer will consider features, but buy on benefits. Do not assume, after you choose the features with which you will fight the mercantile wars, that the benefits of the features are clear.

Unfortunately, if you are the program leader on a project, convincing the foot soldiers of the vision that getting the program done within six months is a make-it-or-break-it proposition will be difficult. It will be harder to convince programmers that you are fighting a strategic battle and need to be better in some, but not all, areas of competition. This is because of the fierce pride of most programmers. Why programmers are emotionally attached to their work requires consideration of the art of computer programming.

Although we refer to programmers as "engineers," implying that they use scientific and industrial principles to create end product, computer programming is still very much a creative art. Operationally, computer programming is closer to hand making furniture than building a blender. Indeed, many of the best computer programmers are musicians because they have an artistic temperament. Whatever the field, "shoot 'em up" games to word processors, computer software development is closer in process to painting a picture than building a car.

If you build a car, clear blueprints and plans show exactly what the end product will look like. In modern manufacturing, a detailed specification will be created for each and every part, meaning that in-house personnel or outsources know exactly what kind of oil filter gasket will go into the final car. However, although you may make a detailed specification of a computer program and a prototype, the actual "blueprints," the source code, won't exist until final delivery. In building the Boeing 777, engineers used three-dimensional computer modeling to build a virtual plane before building the first one on the factory floor. The engineers could resolve "interferences," problems in which parts couldn't be built as specified because of physical obstruction of one another, on screen.

When the design of the first Boeing 777 was finished, all the factory and subcontractors had to do was follow the instructions. Once built, it was possible to do a 100 percent compliance check for variance between the design and real-world program. That's impossible in a computer program of any complexity. This lack of building from a fixed design makes a computer program unlike standard industrial product and brings it back to the realm of fine arts.

As a result, programmers have a proprietary view toward their output. Ask programmers about their dreams, and they'll all mention creating the killer application for (fill in the blank here). Killer applications are programs that are so revolutionary that users adopt that computer platform or paradigm so that they can use that killer app. If you read the history of computer software, you're likely to learn about killer apps like spreadsheets, desktop publishing, or e-mail. Spreadsheets launched PCs, desktop publishing the Mac line of machines, and e-mail is the killer app for the Internet. Convincing a software team to put their effort into preparing a program for the real world of mass market software is a tough job.

Killer apps have to be the best of the best. Nothing in it can be a compromise. Extremes in innovation, usefulness, speed, and interface necessitate heroic efforts, during which the programming team lives on takeout food and super-caffeinated drinks for months and months, emerging with a world killer. It's a beautiful vision, but almost certainly one that is an unattainable goal. Even if you make a program that is the height of the art of computer software engineering, you must have an exact pulse on the public's desires.

One constant in all software management is getting the best from the team. However, mass market software is different from corporate or other development. Although getting the best is a laudable goal, usually getting a B+ effort in half the time of an A effort is better for your project in noncritical areas of the program. As a gun pointed at a person focuses his or her attention, a deadline does the same. We're not creating a prescription for mediocrity. Rather, to be a success, key and essential features must be first class. However, using "canned" components or simple solutions to issues that are not critical to the core of the program speeds development and reduces costs, also gaining the development team the luxury of the flexibility that a quick development cycle provides. However, when you use tools from third parties, even if you get the full source code, you need to be sure that the vendor will be around to support your product. One insider takes the properly paranoid approach of separately compiling the source code that they get with the vendor's tools to verify that they get the same object output as provided by the developer.

Any program that is on the market is better than any potential program — regardless of the ultimate merits of the two programs. A program that is on the market at least has the opportunity to gain loyalty, referrals, and reviews. A potential program can do none of this. Indeed, it seems that many program development teams from the largest publishers use the public as beta testers and assume that the 1.0 release is a loss. You can't get the public's feedback and consumer's feedback without releasing the program. In other words, some programs are released and others escape. Knowing exactly when to let your young take flight is the key.

Reis and Trout, the authors of the *Guerrilla Marketing* series, emphasize that the most critical battle in marketing is for awareness of the product within the mind of the user. Being first on the market gives you the best chance to gain that awareness. If you're not first, seizing the public mind is almost impossible. Microsoft has frequently gone to market with programs that were less than ready for market, knowing they could release better versions later. Microsoft Windows 3.0 wasn't ready for prime time. Nevertheless, Microsoft got the program out, started obtaining the public awareness, and achieved to a virtual hegemony in operating system software. A great deal of that success lies in the fact that Gates took the risk and got the program out.

Since speed is a critical issue, project management must maximize the chances that the program has to successfully meet its deadlines. Classic texts on software development suggest an allocation of total resources as follows:

Feature list, design, prototyping, and acceptance criteria — 25 to 30 percent

Coding and development — 30 to 40 percent

Testing — 30 to 40 percent

The most neglected step is creating a clear design and acceptance benchmark. Every minute spent in planning pays dividends in enforcing discipline to the project. A design must include specific, detailed feature lists that lead to an acceptance benchmark. As each feature is added to the list, an estimate of the amount of time required to complete should be made, even if guesswork is involved. Any interdependencies must be charted. Even advanced programming teams sometimes forget, when creating specifications, to indicate any communication, data access, or other interaction between program functions. Finally, each function should be assigned a priority and relative completion date. If you are dealing with multiple team members, the order in which program functions are completed is quite important so that a programmer who needs to receive data from a particular input menu can begin work with access to that function. By charting the order that program functions need to be completed and double-checking this against a list of interdependencies, you can limit downtime or "waiting for someone else" to get finished. If a program is assigned to a single programmer, having guidance on the order to complete items will organize and streamline completion.

Having an acceptance benchmark is very important because you know when you're done. Experts on software development for the corporate world have discovered that after a program is done, corporate development teams spend time equal to one-fifth of the total development cycle on polishing the deliverable. However, testing shows that when the program was "done," the polishing did not increase user acceptance of the program. Be sure to have a plan for what is good enough, and then *stop*. If your team gains even half of the time apparently wasted on polishing, you will meet tight development deadlines.

From the beginning, you must weigh the importance of every feature you'd like to include in your program against the time it would take to prepare that feature. This will help you decide which time-consuming features can be postponed until the next version, in order to meet your release date. Programmers, given sufficient resources, can code anything. The most critical resource to a developer is time. During the design phase, the programming team must decide how far they will go on each feature. Once the design nears completion, you are able to come to an intelligent and reasoned expectation for what can actually be delivered within the constraints of the real world.

Here's an example of the detail that should be used in creating a design specification for a single function in a program, and the acceptance benchmark. Our test case will be the design of a feature for an Internet babysitting program. Internet babysitters lessen the chance that younger children will be able to access materials on the web that are designed for adults. One feature that will be needed is a timer and rationing system.

Feature 1

Time control preset. The parent will access a menu through a password-protected menu and allocate a specific time allowed for computer use per child. All user input, except for the children's names in the initial entry, will be accomplished through drop-down menus.

After completing a specific feature list and an estimate of the time required for each feature, the tasks can be divided among team members. From that point on, the design should be fixed. The most common reason for a program not shipping on time is that the design is changed. During the design phase of program development, an estimate of time is made for coding and testing each function. Professional programmers consider the interdependencies between various parts of a project and plan accordingly. Last-minute changes cause severe disruptions to the potentially thousands of possible combinations of interaction within programs.

The correct philosophy in testing a program is that if *any* change is made, the program must be completely retested. Even with modular, structured code, one small change can produce side effects in an otherwise stable system.

During the design phase, RAD tools should be used to prototype the program interface. Frequent use of prototypes and demonstrations serve to refine the output and improve the quality of work more dramatically than any other testing process. It's one thing to deal with a list or a specification. With an actual program to use, even if many features are stubbed out, meaningful input can be received from actual users, who are able to judge something much more substantial than a features list.

The discipline of mass market software development subjects a program to more stress than vertical market programs. It is possible to make some reasonable default assumptions regarding the use of standard cards, motherboards, memory, and peripherals when your program is designed for limited release. A program to achieve mass market sales needs to be available and usable by virtually every machine out there.

Mass market programs must meet rigorous goals to have a chance of success. For example, a program that sells a thousand copies with a 1 percent problem with installation, generates ten problems, returns, or support calls. A mass market program that sells 1 million copies and that has a one-tenth of 1 percent failure rate generates a thousand problems. If those one thousand programs are returned, and the program wholesales for $20, it can cost $20,000 plus the paperwork burden related to the returns.

The following are the areas that cause the most problems and need to be reviewed closely. If there is any way to simplify any of these factors, it is vital to do so.

USE A STANDARD INTERFACE

If you develop for Microsoft Windows, purchase a copy of the *User Interface Guidelines*. With other target platforms, obtain the guidelines for their user interfaces. Any investment that you make in using the standard interface for your target operating systems will pay significant dividends in reduced complaints and returns and in customer goodwill. Carefully examine the most popular applications in your chosen target market, and adhere to the standard.

PROVIDE SIMPLICITY OF INSTALLATION

As computer software has to deal with more and more peripheral equipment and variations in operating systems, installation becomes more difficult. Every question that an installer asks is another problem and potential difficulty. Pay attention to potential installation issues early in the design stage.

ALLOW FOR SIMPLICITY OF INTERFACE TO PERIPHERALS

If a program interacts with peripherals, the less the user has to do in order to use the program the better. An example of the best in user interface in peripheral design is the work by Hewlett-Packard. A customer installing a printer or other HP peripheral gets a totally system-compliant installation routine with strong graphics and, at the conclusion, an opportunity to test if the peripheral has been successfully installed using a test print or other report.

OPERATE OUT OF THE BOX

Programs like MS Word demonstrate that the most complicated programs can still be used immediately out of the box with little or no review of manuals and help files. Additionally, users can discover more and more features as they work with the choices in the various menus.

Users of MS Word can start typing as soon as they get the program. Within a relatively short time, they can prepare simple documents. After working with the program, the user can start using each of the program's features without committing to learning complicated commands. This is achieved by the use of drop-down menus and icons that perform related groups of functions. Virtually all levels of complexity can be reached through no more than three or four mouse clicks.

CREATE EXTENSIBILITY

If a program is released within tight time guidelines, some features were probably subject to compromise. Assume over time that competitors will counterfeature or "escalate" by adding in more functionality. As a result, you must create a design that is robust enough to permit the addition of more features. Good mass market programming practice, described in further detail in this chapter, results in a program that can be expanded.

Hundreds of textbooks and articles concern computer software project management. Each has a good point or two, but the field most analogous to mass market software is "real-time" programming, the type of programs that are used in airliners or elevators to run a real-world system. These programs must show the same robustness as mass market software.

Implementation of each of the following design policies will result in a robust design that will excel even if distributed in mass market quantities. These recommendations also speed up development by allocating resources efficiently. Each policy can be implemented in any programming language and any programming paradigm.

RECORD ALL ASSUMPTIONS, AND ELIMINATE AS MANY AS POSSIBLE

Each assumption about what a user knows in terms of the operating system or your interface is a potential source of support calls and lack of user acceptance. If a program assumes certain levels of installed equipment, or system resources, document the assumptions, and seek to eliminate or reduce them. In particular, avoid assumptions about the user's ability to adjust to nonstandard interfaces. By rigorously applying this rule, developers learn that they've made more guesses than they would otherwise suspect. If an assumption is vital, conduct an honest analysis of what market share it may cost you or how many support calls it may cause.

SELF-PROTECT SOFTWARE

If software requires that a printer, modem, or other peripheral be connected and operating, check for the status of the peripheral during initialization. This may be one of the most commonly neglected engineering habits. Your software will be a better value to your users if it does the error checking first, not last. For example, if a program sends faxes, check if the fax is connected before converting the computer file to a fax. An error message indicating that the fax machine isn't operative is an annoyance after the conversion. It's much better to tell the user "verify that the fax is on" before converting a complicated graphic to a fax rather than after. There are very simple algorithms to verify that your executable and any needed support files are uncorrupted and located in the right place on the system. Interrupt the user to let him or her know that a file is missing before, rather than after, he or she begins working. Finally, check for system memory and resources before starting the program, and warn the user that he or she needs to close other applications so that work flow is not interrupted.

INCLUDE DIAGNOSTICS

Any customer forced to call for support probably isn't thrilled and may not buy updates. Your customer will be happier, and your bottom line better if support calls are short. Include a diagnostic routine in your program that checks anything that your program requires or that you assumed would be available. Given that you have an assumptions list, program a menu feature to check that all the system assumptions you made are true. If customers can access and read system information to you immediately, their time on the phone to the support desk, and your support staff time, will be optimized. Here are a few concrete examples. If certain dynamic link libraries or drivers are required, write a diagnostic routine that "greps" (grep, or global regular expression parser, is a command that searches files for text you are looking for) the system and verifies the existence of the files, their location, and the system path. Your customer support desk can get this information faxed or called in and immediately determine whether the problem is a missing or corrupt file rather than playing the customer-support "20 Questions" game. Lack of disk space also can cause strange errors. Include a diagnostic for the number of allocation units and absolute space available, and your help desk can get to this potential source of error quickly.

CREATE MEANINGFUL ERROR MESSAGES

"Unsupported device" and "bad command or file name" are poor error messages. They do not help the user help themselves. If possible, an error message should include enough information so that the user can refer to the manual for a fix that he or she can perform. Anyone who has worked a support desk knows that people don't check their manuals very often. However, if you explain to a customer that fixing the error was anticipated and is in the manual, the customer's faith in the program returns. Finally, each error message should refer to the sections of the user's guide that explain how the errors occur and how to prevent them from recurring.

ANTICIPATE ERRORS AND PROVIDE SOLUTIONS

Consider every inappropriate action that a user may take, like changing the location of files needed to operate the program. Users frequently take actions that excellent software engineering can't anticipate, such as adding more hard drives or changing the logical location of needed files from D: to E:. Provide a frequently asked questions (FAQ) file suggesting solutions to user-inflicted errors, such as problems that will arise if the user reconfigures the system without changing the program's installation. As noted, when errors occur, provide an error message containing a solution and a reference to the user's guide.

INTERNATIONALIZE AND ACCOMMODATE DISABILITIES

Software is now a world market. Place your string literals in container files, and read them into the program so that the bulk of translation can be undertaken in one file. Keep in mind that blind users, or users with problems with their extremities, will use mass market programs. Governments and other large organizations may condition acceptance of your program on accommodating those with disabilities. There are added bonuses to placing strings in container files. Changes to the original version are more quickly made. In addition, a program that reads in strings can be rebranded and reused to create different-appearing programs to allow multiple channel marketing. Functions, procedures, and methods that don't have strings embedded in them are more easily reused, facilitating reuse of code.

RELEASE ALL MEMORY USED

If your program allocates memory, be sure to deallocate it. This error is prevalent in most object-oriented programs, including flagship programs from the largest publishers. Language constructions are available that force programs to return to functions so as to release system resources no longer needed.

MINIMIZE USE OF "GLOBAL" VARIABLES

If a global variable is created and its value is modified so that it is wrong and causes an error, any module, procedure, or function in the program can be the source of the error. Bug fixing is greatly protracted. Pass values rather than rely on the use of global variables.

CREATE A ROBUST PROGRAM, THEN OPTIMIZE SPEED

"Speed kills!" Program functions should be coded for maximum reliability. After design for reliability is completed, tools are available to determine which functions in the program are taking the most time. These alone should be recoded for speed. Writing an entire program, or even major components, maximized for speed requires significantly more time than coding for reliability. Besides taking more time to write, programs designed for speed consume more system resources and use shortcuts that are more likely to produce bugs than code made for reliability. This policy can significantly shorten development cycles.

VERIFY ALL INPUT

Any user input should be checked for reasonableness and for allowable values before it is processed by the system. Fortunately, most development environments contain "picture" or "mask" features that encourage the user to enter valid input. Great computer engineering assists the user in entering appropriate input. For example, rather than typing in dates, show the current date, and then allow the user to access the months and years via drop-down menus or similar conventions. This work will prevent the user from entering an invalid date and helps him or her use the program more quickly. The user and developer benefit since this system incorporates input validation and gives the user meaningful feedback.

USE MANUAL AND AUTOMATED TESTING

Every function should be hand-tested by a programmer, preferably someone other than the programmer who created it, by taking both reasonable and unreasonable inputs and manually following execution of the code. Industry and academic studies show that code that is proofread by another programmer for logic and syntax errors lets far fewer errors into testing and production. A useful side effect of this practice is that code must be written in a clearly commented and logical fashion. Automated testing suites are available that provide truly exhaustive testing of developers' programs.

LIMIT NESTING

Programming lends itself to multiple levels of nested commands. Many years of reviewing source code show that programmers may go five or more levels deep in "switch" or "if-then-else" statements. This type of coding causes some of the hardest errors to catch. Excessive levels of "nesting" make other good practices like hand-executing code and code inspection much more difficult. Constructs this complex have too many places where something can go wrong. Find more elegant and readable solutions to these programming issues that further subdivide functions.

OBTAIN ISO CERTIFICATION

The "total quality" and "reengineering" principles have gone from buzz words to real innovations and improvements in many industries. The rediscovery of Deming's principles has reinvigorated many industries. Deming's idea is that through true participative factory management, defects and rework can be minimized, resulting in tremendous savings in manufacturing and customer service. In 1987, the International Standards Organization adopted the ISO 9000 series of specifications for certification of quality control. More than 140 countries recognize ISO quality certification, using essentially the same standards. At the time that this is being written, ISO 9000 certification has not become a vital competitive factor in North America. However, in the international markets, and in Europe in particular, certification is encouraged and recognized as necessary for successfully competing. ISO certification is, however, recognized by both governments and large businesses within North America as important for dealing with governmental, industrial, and export customers.

Three different certifications apply to publishers of software:

1. ISO 9001 Quality System Model for Quality Assurance in Design/Development, Production, Installation and Services. This standard applies to any organization that provides products or services designed to meet a standard (as opposed to providing products that are ungraded, like fine art pieces). ISO 9001 is the base certification required. An organization that seeks international quality standard approval will have to implement controls in more than twenty areas. These include quality system, design control, document control, inspection and testing, corrective standards, quality documentation records, and internal audits.

   Being a supplier of mass market software certification under ISO 9001 provides a competitive advantage in selling to governmental, business, and export customers.

2. ISO 9000-3 deals specifically with certification of software organizations under Section 9100. Three broad categories are covered: framework, life cycle, and support. Framework covers management and internal quality control. Life cycle is concerned with design, testing, and maintenance of code. Support covers tools and techniques, use of external software products, and training.

3. ISO 9004-2 sets standards for customer support.

Any organization that has completed the processes required to achieve certification has established an institutional ethos of quality and inspection.

There are three modes of ISO certification: first party (self-assessment), second party (used by one party to assure quality of another), and third party (independent review of an organization leading to certification). Each of these modes is important in conducting international business.

Organizations certified under ISO 9000 must ensure that their subcontractors and suppliers follow proper quality control, either by being ISO certified or through a review of the subcontractor's quality control. An ISO-certified organization must use tools, like computer software, that are certified by the user to be of acceptable quality.

Over time, ISO certification will become more common worldwide, and will probably become a requirement for mass market sales.

CHAPTER 4

▷ Pricing, Packaging, and Profit Centers

This chapter will cover several closely related topics. Pricing, packaging, and profit centers are the factors most vital to the success or failure of your program. Too many great ideas were "dead on arrival" because of poor price point, poor packaging, and failure to obtain the most revenue from each sale.

While interviewing prominent insiders for this book, I was surprised to find a level of secrecy that I hadn't anticipated. Many people were willing to share the secrets of their companies' success, but few were willing to go on the record. The distributors and retailers whom I interviewed exhibited an incredibly high degree of reticence when I asked about their policies on reviewing the programs that they eventually purchased or promoted. The only topic that insiders agreed upon unanimously was that manufacturer's representatives and buyers do *not* run programs before buying them. In fact, when I asked about this, I was besieged by requests not to quote anyone specifically about this fact. Packaging is what sells your program, and packaging determines whether it succeeds or fails. As noted, software publishing has much in common with book publishing, and like books, software is sold by the cover.

It was clear to me that everyone within the industry knows that once a publisher has packaged a program, its fate is determined by that packaging and pricing. However, it seems that insiders are ashamed of this fact, but they shouldn't be so defensive. Given the environment in which software is sold, it makes a great deal of sense that they would treat the software as a commodity. Software is wholesaled on a returnable basis. Every publisher puts its reputation — and its cash — behind its releases. There is an unspoken assumption that the goods are marketable. Wholesale buyers assume that the publishers already have winnowed out any poor programs. Additionally, many retailers carry thousands of titles, and unless they hired at least dozens of software testers, they have to accept the publishers' representation that the programs work and are worth at least as much as the manufacturer wants to charge.

Unfortunately, this assumption is not always accurate. Particularly, but not exclusively, in lower-priced lines, there is rampant overpackaging. Too many programs packaged in large boxes contain only a single CD in a tyvek sleeve, not even in a jewel case. Programs packaged in boxes have room to include a printed manual, but many developers have adopted a policy of selling CD-ROM titles in box format without even a small printed user manual. However good the online documentation might be, many end users cannot confidently use online help. In particular, end users need written guidance on installation just to get as far as the online help. If you can't afford even a small user's guide, you are trying to squeeze too much profit out of the transaction.

If your exterior packaging and presentation are great, but the inside is cheap, customers feel cheated. You can forget developing customer goodwill, or selling to the same customer again. Overpackaged software not only irritates customers, it also undermines that most valuable company asset, customer goodwill. If you want to make maximum profits, your goal must be to do business many times with the same customers. You want them to think as highly of your software *after* they've gotten the product home and opened the box.

Packaging is an art practiced by graphic and fine artists whose training is equivalent in length and depth to that of computer programmers. Like most experts, they know a great deal about a very specialized area. You must hire the best artists and packaging designers.

Acquire an assortment of your competitors' programs, and examine their packaging. Compare your packaging side by side with theirs. Remember that your potential customers will hold your box in one hand, and your competitor's in their other hand. Do the same comparison. What does your competitor highlight? Does your packaging compare well, or do you need to highlight different selling points?

Visit retailers, and try to visualize where your program may be physically placed. How would your package attract attention? One close friend experienced great success by following a simple rule: make sure that your package can be seen from thirty feet away. Talk with your graphic designer and use gold foil or other eye-catching schemes. The few extra cents per unit that superior packaging costs can make the difference between returns or sell through.

All is lost if your A+ program is in a D- box. Spend extra to get the highest-quality packaging and printing. Your program's sleeve or jewel case software is your only way to communicate your quality to most buyers, particularly at the point of purchase. Users equate excellent packaging with excellent content.

Quality, features, and reliability are important factors in selling computer programs. Design your packaging to stress a few clear advantages of your software. Remember, unless properly explained and communicated on the packaging, those advantages will have no effect on your sales.

The job of graphic design for computer program packages has been made considerably more difficult by the retail trend to sell software in jewel cases. The jewel case has an extremely small "canvas" on which to effectively communicate your strengths, differentiation, and features. Some publishers use the same art on both the jewel case and boxed product. Although simply shrinking the box art onto the jewel case (or blowing up the jewel case art to fit the box) sounds like a quick and easy way to design all of your packaging at once, it's not a good idea.

If there is one overriding theme throughout the future of retailing, it is that people will have less and less time. Shopping must be done faster, but at the same time, customers demand higher quality. The amount of copy that you can work with on a jewel box is less than you can get onto software in a cardboard package. Your packaging must have an immediate, compelling effect on end users.

For your packaging to be compelling, you must understand the distinction between features and benefits. As developers, we put a great deal of effort into planning and then programming the features of our programs. Features are very important to us. We define our work flow and accomplishments by features. But our customers think in terms of benefits to them. Let's begin by examining the difference between features and benefits on a noncomputer item that we are all familiar with — the microwave oven.

Features
800 watts power, turntable carousel, programmable cpu, insertable thermocouple

---

Unless you are a microwave oven expert, these features may mean little to you and would probably fail to influence your purchasing decision. But recast as benefits, these same features become powerful sales tools.

Benefits
The microwave has a high power level, so it will quickly cook all of your meals. Your food will be evenly cooked because the microwave has a carousel that automatically turns. With the programmable cpu, you are able to set the microwave in advance so that it will start and stop cooking while you are at work. With the thermometer, you'll be able to cook food to the precise temperature that you want. Cooking to a precise temperature eliminates guesswork so the meals will be cooked perfectly every time.

Benefits are how the features that you have put in your product have a positive impact on the desires of your customers. Explaining the features to the customers in terms of the benefits to them makes the second hypothetical microwave oven sound much more appealing than the first one, which was described in terms of features only. Salespeople may do well with features, but close the sale on benefits.

Packaging can describe features, but it must be done in a way that demonstrates the benefit to the customer. After all, a significant number of computer users, which amounts to a significant part of the mass market, are "feature aware." Magazines and their reviewer writers love to compare lists of features — particularly since it's one of the only "objective measures" that can be used in an otherwise subjective judgment of how well a program compares to others.

In this environment, your packaging must make an immediate impact, but you will have less time than ever before in which to make it. As noted in Chapter 10, you must pick a single issue or unique selling point, and then define the battle for market share in those terms so that you can fight the war on your terms. Remember, most purchases, particularly software purchases, are made on impulse, so if you make your strengths sound better than the other program's, you can close the sale rapidly.

The term *packaging* also refers to an entirely different issue: using the same code to make different products. Many developers have reached a million sales by using a software engine that can be reconfigured, or that can have additional data added to it, to create a new program. Likewise, a program can be downsized to a "lite" version to fit into other markets.

My legal guide series was developed as a general-purpose document creation program. It has been used as the basis for several other document-creating products that have earned yet more revenue, significantly leveraging the investment in development. Take the time to add in code to make a general-purpose program rather than a single-purpose application, and you will be able to earn additional revenue.

Many people thought that Desilu Studios was crazy to want to hold onto the right for residual income from "I Love Lucy Show" repeats. However, Lucy's programs are still being rerun, and payments are still being made to the owner of the programs. Developers of computer programs must take the same attitude. During the negotiation of a book or magazine article assignment, authors or their agents at least recognize that a work of intellectual property has many potential markets. Rarely are "all world" rights sold.

In the usual give and take in coming to a business deal to publish a work, some rights are demanded by each party. Here's a nonexhaustive list of rights available in any intellectual property:

- First publication

- Reprint in whole or in abridgments

- Rights by territory (United States and Canada; all countries except for Japan, and so on)

- Translation rights to different languages

- Translation rights to different means of viewing or using the work (television, radio, movie, CD-ROM, multimedia)

- Rights to improved or expanded versions

- Rights to discrete parts of the work: for example, in a computer program, rights to a particular subfunction or, in a computer program with original art, the right to publish the art in a medium other than computers

- Rights measured by number of years (three years United States)

- Rights to particular markets defined by price point

- Nonexclusive publication

When dealing with potential publishing partners, insist that if they want a particular right that they exploit it. For example, it isn't reasonable for a publisher to demand exclusive publication rights worldwide if the publisher has no distributors in some parts of the world or a bona fide plan to establish overseas distribution.

In regard to price point, channel conflict does not exist between $400 and $10 programs. So long as there is differentiation between the programs' names and features, it is again not reasonable to demand rights that are not going to be used.

You are not selling a program; rather, you are publishing or licensing a specific programming package. Each repackaging is a new opportunity although you should observe any limits that prevent a legitimate channel conflict.

As noted in Chapter 5, all retail space requires an entry fee in the form of slotting fees, free goods, or other allowances. Since the charge for this space is supported by the marketplace, there is a clear value for the simple right to occupy the space. "Real estate" is prized, and the most recent trend in the software business is for retailers to carry fewer SKUs (acronym for bar-code — one item for sale in a store).

Therefore, good business practice demands that the investment in shelf space be managed for maximum return. Having gone through all the steps to get a program on the market, the real estate inside the box needs to be used as well. Upgrades and updates should be a profit center that makes the developer more than the profit on the original sale did. After all, you can sell several generations of updates or improved programs to customers. Every expert in the area of sales and marketing agrees that it is cheaper and more profitable to do more business with your existing customers than it is to prospect and close new customers. Here are some of the most commonly used strategies for doing repeat business.

BOUNCEBACKS AND UPGRADES

To make the greatest financial success of your product, you must be creative. Make new editions of your program that can be offered as upgrades to the retail program the customers have purchased. The offer should be a good one, yet not lead the customers to believe that they have been sold a poor program for the sole purpose of pitching an upgrade to the "real" thing. The best upgrades are for "more of the same" rather than for additional features. Thus, if you have a collection of recipes, a great upgrade is a collection of additional recipes rather than an upgrade that uses the same data, but offers more functionality.

One way to get the best response is to "credit" the customer with the manufacturer's suggested retail price (MSRP) of the program that they have already purchased. For example, if your update price is $99, and the MSRP of the original program is $29, sell the upgrade for $70. After all, you've cut out the middleman, and the end users will not think that they wasted their original investment in the program. The easiest way to understand this concept is that you don't want the customers to believe that they should have purchased the upgrade instead of the program that they did purchase.

SALES OF SPACE IN PACKAGES

Since retailers sell space in the store, software entrepreneurs can sell inserts, demonstration disks, or other marketing materials in their packaging to third parties. Some software developers have made their boxes into temples of commerce, and dozens of offers fall out of every box. This is a terrible deal for those who purchase inserts since individual offers will get less of the customers' attention. Long-term relationships, in which the publisher and insert advertiser refine the offers to increase buyer response, are the most profitable arrangements.

There are a number of ways to sell insertions. The most traditional type of insert is a booklet or card for an affinity product. These are sold either as per inquiry or as flat rate compensation. A per inquiry payment, also called a per sale arrangement, is made each time someone buys an item. Sales are tracked either on a trust basis, where the insert company uses code numbers to track where sales referrals originated, or by having the orders pass through the software publisher, or by receiving a report from a third party like an answering service. Standard Rate and Data Service provides a listing of insertion opportunities and pricing. Study this publication, available at libraries, to learn the rates charged for different types of inserts.

Typical response rates vary from one in a thousand (one-tenth of 1 percent), for the most general products, to five or six in a thousand (six-tenths of 1 percent), for more narrowly targeted or "closely coupled" offers. Insiders believe that the closer the coupling, the higher the return. Using this logic, the strongest candidate for affinity sales would be add-ons to the program itself. However, like a great deal of the industry wisdom, this relationship is anecdotal rather than scientific.

In too many cases, response languishes in the one in a thousand range because the offers are not strong enough to motivate customers to make a decision to purchase, or even to request further information. Offers that traditionally have done the best are the "free issue — cancel if not satisfied" offers for magazines and the like.

SERVICE CONTRACTS

The original computer software support was toll-free support, which forced computer programs to retail at very high prices in order to amortize the support costs within the purchase price. Most programs now offer some support in the first thirty days, after which 900-line or other charges apply. Another variation on this theme is a permanent relationship, in which for a yearly fee the customer receives updates, upgrades, and preferred support for a product or product line. These ongoing support contracts can also include priority access to support or use of 800 numbers to reach technical support. A good support and automatic upgrade system is a win–win situation for the developer and customer.

MAILING LISTS

The rental of mailing lists is a significant source of income for some companies with mailing lists of at least five thousand persons. More money is paid for the names of the most recent customers. Renting mailing lists is a highly specialized field.

SUPPLIES

In the areas of accounting software and desktop publishing software, there are natural tie-ins for consumable supplies. Paper and forms are a very profitable business. The suppliers of consumables are always interested in obtaining new customers and are willing to share profits with computer program suppliers. This can include direct tie-ins or more sophisticated arrangements.

PRICING

The final ingredient in packaging is pricing. Poor decisions concerning pricing have killed more promising titles than any other mistake made by developers. Unfortunately, there is no formula to use to determine what pricing will produce the highest return on investment. In many cases, the seemingly contradictory is true: often a lower price produces more profit than a higher one.

On the other hand, perceived value is still an issue in software marketing although less of one than in the past. The concept of perceived value is that customers assume that a higher-priced item must contain more value than a lower-priced one. Although this may be true in standard commodities, software is one of the fields in which there is virtually no correspondence between price and quality. In the early days of mass market software, many programs in the lower-priced ranges were indeed much worse on any objective standard than the better established programs. As the software market has matured, the difference between a $9 and $49 program is often little or nothing other than the goals or business plan of the developer. Because software is intangible, subjective issues of taste enter into the determination of what is "better." As the customers become more and more sophisticated, they are discovering that price is a function of marketing rather than a reflection of intrinsic worth.

Despite the uncertainty that surrounds pricing, mass market items (with a few exceptions) must be sold as impulse items, as we have described in Chapter

5. In the present marketplace, programs above $29.95 have a significantly worse chance of making it to mass market status than do those below $29.95. In fact, if you examine sales figures provided by independent firms that monitor sales, with very few exceptions, sales of comparable applications begin to drop significantly above a $14.95 street price. Ego aside, to reach mass market success and earn the large financial rewards, don't do anything that interferes with your end user's impulse decision making. Whatever price you are considering, go to the lowest price at which you can still make a profit, and watch your volume grow. Hedge your bets by limited releases of higher-priced software or upgrades.

PART II

▷ **Market
Development**

CHAPTER 5

▷ Retail Distribution

As this book is being written, retail sales is the primary way that computer applications software is sold. This includes OEM bundling in machines sold at mail order or retail. The retail channel can be further subdivided into VARs (Value Added Retailer), superstores, malls, mass merchandisers, warehouse clubs, and nontraditional outlets. Whether your software is published by another, self-published, or bundled, a good grasp of the realities of retail sales of computer programs is required to be able to successfully judge the effectiveness of your partners.

As a successful software entrepreneur you will have to push lots of product through each distribution method. From time to time, software developers ignore one distribution method so that they can concentrate on others. But each method has a share in the balance of power, and even though some developers have favored just one channel, each time the equilibrium restored itself. No software developer has succeeded over the long term in trying to change the balance.

Remember your emotional state when you learned that there was no Santa Claus? Prepare yourself for a similar shock. When dealing with retailers, you will be selling your program *solely* on a feature list, sell sheet, catalog entry, or mockup of the box. Unless the buyer has a particular interest in the program, your program will be bought and sold, be a success or failure, based on packaging. Having gone through this rite of passage you now know that the most important part of your effort, after selecting your title and price point, is the quality of packaging and art. Forget this at the peril of being one of the many who fail at mass market software, not the few who create big winners.

Your entry into retailing must also be guided by the fact that 85 percent of computer program purchases are made on impulse. Out of every one hundred programs that you sell, eighty-five will be to persons who had no intention of buying a computer program at all. Computer software is a secretive business, and one in which many truths are known only to the initiated. The fact that software is an impulse item is one of them. Insiders don't like to go on record about the demographics of their purchasers or what types of titles they think will be most successful. In fact, no buyer, merchandise manager, or vice president of merchandising agreed to go on record for this book.

The industry profile for purchasers of computer software is that the modal purchaser is male, in his thirties to forties, married with children, and purchasing for his own use. Our typical buyer has some college education and has an average household income of well over $60,000. However, the dispersal and variation among individual titles is so high that it is not statistically meaningful to try to generalize. Your purchasers will vary across the entire spectrum of the 30 percent of households with computers.

However simple it may appear to the customer buying a copy of a program from a retail location, placing product in the retail channel is a very complicated process. You might assume that the manufacturer sold the program to a wholesaler who then sold to a retailer, or that the manufacturer sold the product directly to the store. Instead, it is a much more complicated process. Products that are side by side within the same store may have arrived there from rack jobbers, traditional wholesalers, manufacturer direct, or two types of nontraditional wholesalers. You may be surprised to find that every SKU in the store, whether a one-location "mom and pop" store or one of a 2,000-strong store chain, may have arrived at the store through a different distribution method.

So many different types of distribution are used because software is a new industry, and the different retailers who existed before the retail sales of computers and computer software didn't know how to classify software. Therefore, retailers patterned software after goods that they thought were related to software. Some retailers regarded computer software as electronics, others as records or videos, and a few as a new category in itself. Additionally, computer software distribution pioneers Ingram Micro and Handleman came in from book and rack jobbing, respectively, and they brought their world view to the distribution of the new product.

Getting to retail also requires a significant investment in cash. In some cases, the expense of simply obtaining shelf space can exceed the cost of product development. The high costs of entry into the retail channel have driven many computer software companies to develop strategies to try to "get around" retailers, and although a few very successful programs have avoided, or have very creative ways to get around, the problems we'll discuss, you will have to sell successfully at retail if you want to reach seven digits in profitable sales.

As you read this chapter, you may decide that you'd like to find ways to change the balance of power; however, very few programs have ever made it to the million sales mark without retail sales. Retail placement is above all a form of advertising and an affirmation that the "experts" in the market consider the program to be worthy. It is also a form of "referential endorsement." By sitting on the shelves near similar applications, the program shows the public that it's as worthy of consideration as the other programs. Although you may not close the sale at retail, the product being seen in stores can lead to a sale later in another venue.

A product will travel from manufacturer to retail in one of these ways:

- Manufacturer direct

- Traditional wholesale

- Special order wholesale

- Dump bin and "distressed" merchandise

- Nontraditional distributors

The available shelf space and developer's capital decides the method. If a developer has adequate capital to go direct, most will choose to do so. If a particular party, like a wholesaler or rack jobber, obtains all the available shelf space, the developer must go through that organization to get the software into the store. Newer developers will usually have to try to get a foothold in the market through distributors; we will discuss some interesting ways around that in the chapters regarding OEM and shareware.

Even though there are many different ways that the product can arrive in the store, there are some constants, or at least traditions, in the sales of computer programs.

Because software is both electronic and publishing, and it requires electronic equipment to be used, some of the sales and credit terms from consumer electronics apply. In many cases, the terms for sale of computer hardware foreshadow the terms for sale of computer software. But since software is a relatively new type of commodity, in some cases the product will be treated administratively by a retailer as electronics, sometimes as entertainment, and other times as its own area. Further, since computer software is similar to a book, some of the sales and credit terms from the "paper" book trade also apply to software.

If you are an expert on the practices in the book trade, you will find this discussion to be very familiar. The key sales term that has carried over from the book trade is that software is returnable. Almost every sale made by a product supplier to a retailer or wholesaler is not final. The retailer, or wholesaler, can return unsold inventory to the party that they acquired the program from, whether a wholesaler or the manufacturer. In almost all cases, there is a disincentive for returns: the retailer or wholesaler has to pay shipping in both directions.

The right of return may be formally set by a "turn rate." If the program meets the turn rate, it stays in stock and is reordered. On the other hand, if the turn rate isn't met, the unsold programs can be returned. Required turn rates vary from retail outlet to retail outlet, but some rough average minimums are:

1.5 to 2 sales per store month — computer specialty stores

2 sales per store month — general mass merchandisers

3 to 6 sales per store month — superstores and warehouse clubs

Even though selling two programs or so per store month seems to be a relatively easy goal to meet, most programs fall below this rate during the first two or three months after placement.

"Hit programs" that have the chance to make a million or more sales generally average sell throughs directly related to the sales price regardless of the type of outlet, selling more at retailers featuring lower prices to the customers:

10 to 20 per store month — superstores and warehouse clubs

5 to 10 per store month — street price retailers

3 to 10 per store month — MSRP retailers

If there is no formal policy on turn rates, the retailer may nevertheless obtain the right to return stock by not reordering unless the stock is balanced by taking back slower-moving goods. Whatever contracts may provide, a retailer does not have to reorder or renew an arrangement if the retailer is displeased with the sales performance of the goods initially purchased.

There are horror stories about returns. These include sales that were made as "nonreturnable" that turned into returns for "defective goods." You'd be surprised how much damage a few eight year olds can do with hammers in a warehouse. Another is returns of products that were never placed on the shelf.

Returns are a funny animal for another reason. The price that a retailer or wholesaler pays for programs has to include the risk that the manufacturer perceives for returns. True "no return" arrangements, where even the risk of eight year olds destroying the merchandise is low, always have a lower price than sales that do allow returns. Some customers have obtained a reputation for being so good at retailing that they rarely return the products they sell. As a result, their cost is lower, giving them an advantage when attracting consumers, or a higher profit margin, depending on whether or not they pass price savings on to customers.

Computer hardware manufacturers have been fighting returns as a major drain on profits, in particular, after the 1991 revelation that Packard Bell had a return rate of 20 percent of its total sales. Hardware manufacturers have now successfully negotiated caps with their dealers varying from 10 to 5 percent. Using a carrot as well as a stick, some large hardware manufacturers have added yearly rebates ranging from 1 percent of sales to as much as 3 percent if retailers meet goals for returns. For example, IBM has offered hardware retailers who do not return products a rebate of 1 percent of wholesale sales. Since large publicly held retailers have profit margins of 13 percent or so, a rebate of 1 percent of the cost of their hardware purchases adds a lot to the bottom line.

Although at this time only a few large developers have succeeded in instituting return caps of about 10 percent, given the historic relationship between electronic hardware and software sales terms, the odds favor that software manufacturers will be able to offer incentives to significantly reduce returns.

Large paper book chains have discovered that it may be better to handle remainders themselves. Some book chains have recently started to purchase best-sellers on a nonreturnable basis and have passed on the savings to their customers, particularly reading club members. For example, some book chains now sell top-ten best-sellers at 40 percent under the cover price — very close to the traditional discount given by wholesalers to retailers. In other cases, the parties agree on disposal of goods in place by progressively discounting unsold goods in the stores.

Egghead, known as a higher-priced, service-based store, recently opened a prototype, a new concept of a "superstore-sized" (24,000 feet, about the size of a smaller Office Depot) store just to sell older and returned goods. The jury is still out, but since distributors of older and close-out software have historically done well, applying the present logic of "bigger is better" means if the superstore is successful for Egghead, others will appear providing an interesting new market and series of alternatives for developers and retailers.

A kinder, gentler form of price protection is stock balancing. Under stock balancing, the retailer or wholesaler may return goods that have not sold, but must take an equal number of other titles in replacement.

A second species of returns are for programs that are sold but returned. Many retailers have signs stating that they "do not accept software returns and make exchanges only." However, despite the risk of dishonesty through customers' copying software and returning it, software is usually accepted for returns if the customer is insistent. One of the most recent trends is to allow a "field destroy" privilege for a certain percentage of defective goods, usually 2 percent. Because of the cost of paperwork for handling piece by piece returns, a field destroy privilege can again be a win–win transaction.

The manufacturer's retail price was an important number at one time in the general world of retailing, and actually was often the sales price. During the 1980s MSRP of computer software became nominal. This is a manifestation of the emergence of deep discounters as a real force in retail sales. To make discounts appear even bigger, most manufacturers raised MSRPs to make the actual, intended street price look like a bargain. Virtually every retailer started discounting from the MSRP. MSRP became meaningless to the customer, except as a guide to the category that a program fit in. MSRP remains important only to the manufacturer and retailers because the whole-sale price is based on a discount of the stated MSRP.

There are two other traditional business terms. The first is "price protection." In the event that your program's price is lowered, you usually must credit the price difference to the retailers who still have product. This was caused by the volatility of pricing for early computers. In the earliest days of the sale of micro-computers, overnight price drops of 95 percent or more were common, resulting in retailers having millions and millions of dollars of overpriced inventory.

Price protection is a valid concept from the retailers' point of view. The computer market is very efficient at distributing information, and even small variations in price are immediately noticed by end users. From a realistic point of view, if you drop your wholesale price, the value of the inventory held by the retailer drops accordingly. Customers also expect that prices will drop over time due to the inherent obsolescence of technology. Publications like the *Computer Shopper* demonstrate that prices of almost everything drop even monthly, or if the price doesn't drop, then performance increases at the same price.

Price protection requires that retailers receive a credit or refund if the MSRP is decreased. Since the retailer can buy from others who have access to the lower-priced identical items, the older inventory is less valuable. These credits are handled as credits in the accounts between the parties or as a cash refund.

The second traditional business term is *version protection*. Since old versions of software can frequently be used to upgrade to new versions of the same program, liquidators often succeeded in selling their programs as tickets to get discounted upgrades to higher versions, so a few developers sold their stock to liquidators with the provision that the software could not be used to upgrade. On the other hand, since most software developers want new relationships with customers so that they can sell yet more upgrades in the future, this is not common.

A recent variation on providing version protection has been placing heavy rebates on older versions or liquidation of the product on site by issuing a credit to the retailer, which is then passed on to the customer. By putting the merchandise on "sale," both the retailer and developer attempt to move the product out of the store to avoid further price protection and to clear the space on the shelf for new goods. As a developer, any steps that lessen the total amount of price protection are money in the bank.

Every aspect of the sale of the product is set by agreement. Since 85 percent of all sales are made as impulse purchases, the emphasis on all promotions should be in increasing the apparent value to the customer of the program at point of sale. This includes:

- Placement of the product, such as spine in or face out, together with specifics regarding location in the store

- Additional point of sale promotion

- Promotion of the product through recommendations or publications

- Promotion of the product through cooperative advertising

- Promotion of the product to the sales personnel working in the stores

- Limited-time special promotions

PLACEMENT OF THE PRODUCT

Product placement within the store can be the difference between selling out and returns. General merchandise stores clearly have good and bad areas. The top shelf space is fought for between competing merchandise. "End caps," which are displays located at the ends of aisles, are special prizes since customers don't have to go down aisles to see those goods.

A contract for retail sale should specify the type of placement. Is the product going to be face out or spine out? Will it occupy a specific slot or be in a communal bin or on a table of mixed goods? What is the stock level? At what point does the retailer reorder? How long will you have the shelf space? Can you engage in stock balancing on your own initiative?

Locations near the cashiers are great. Even whether your product is located at eye level or on the bottom shelf is important. In-store merchandising and display dramatically affect sales results. "Power wings," steel racks that hang off the ends of aisles (like an end cap but to the side), are also considered to be premium space. Retailing legend has it that some floor locations are "power aisles," whereas other aisles aren't. All aspects of how the goods are displayed should be considered and negotiated.

After negotiating for specific placement, the developer should also check for compliance by the retailer. The most successful retailers have the highest rate of compliance with shelving commitments. Other retailers have difficulty in following through on the store-by-store level on commitments made by their home office. A large retail chain recently closed many locations because, insider gossip suggests, some stores were operated by "rogue managers" who put up displays wherever or whenever they felt that it was good for their store.

The deeper question is what to do if there is a lack of compliance. A vendor must always consider that the purchaser need not place any more orders. Therefore, you have to decide how far to push if there is a failure to give you the placement that you contracted for. Even if there is compliance, some sort of cost–benefit analysis in regard to expenditures for placement is necessary. Therefore, if possible, a base-line sales level with a standard, default placement should be reached, and then promotions tried to see if the additional expenditure in obtaining premium space is worth the investment.

Another industry issue is removal of physical product from the shelves. Some stores want to display acrylic-sealed boxes rather than the actual merchandise. The "take a ticket to buy the item" plan may reduce shrink, but estimates range that this decreases sales from 50 to 70 percent compared to giving the customer the tactile experience of handling the box itself. By this logic, of course, you reduce theft to zero by not selling the product at all. A retail chain that is committed to software being displayed this way can nevertheless, through negotiation and at a price, be persuaded to provide a separate display of your goods as stocked items rather than as a "take a ticket" item.

ADDITIONAL POINT OF SALE PROMOTION

Special signs (shelf talkers) or posters or other materials at the point of sale can be negotiated from almost all retailers when placing product in their stores. As with getting space in end caps or power wings, whether or not it is profitable can be determined only by a test marketing of the promotion.

Beginning in early 1996, rebates became a more important part of the computer software scene. Most rebates seemed to be for the purpose of moving out older inventory on site. A number of developers provided rebates to specific stores for thirty- to forty-five-day-long periods. In most cases, these were "upsale" rebates in which the customer was given a rebate for buying two programs from the same line. These promotions are similar in effect to physically wrapping two products together and selling the bundle for the price of one although it has the benefit that the developer gets a mailing list out of the deal. In other cases, rebates were even more targeted, requiring the purchase of two specific titles to get the rebate, not just any two titles from one line. This type of tying arrangement may not have its desired effect since even offering it at a significant discount, people may not want the second, slower-selling title. The jury is out on this case.

More and more retail outlets are providing demonstration machines that allow users to see screen shots, and possibly even perform some simple tasks on the programs in the store. If a demonstration machine is available, be sure to obtain placement on these machines. As an alternative, retailers are creating web sites where demonstration programs or online slide shows are available.

Several concepts have not yet been used but should be. The first is "instant discounting." Under an instant discounting promotion, the price for programs drops with the number purchased, for example:

One program at $9.95

Two programs at $14.95

Three programs at $19.99

This type of promotion requires that the point of sale terminals be programmed to automatically lower the price as more programs from the same company are purchased.

Another is a tie-in between programs and consumables. Some companies "give away" paper with desk-top publishers, but there is also a natural tie-in between desktop publishing and laser printer toner. These tie-ins should be exploited, and as the industry matures, they will be.

PROMOTION OF THE PRODUCT THROUGH RECOMMENDATIONS OR PUBLICATIONS

Several magazines, including *PC Novice*, prepare special "free in store" issues of their magazines aimed at influencing buyers on the spot. These free magazine offers are financed by purchasing ad space in the magazine. Special issues are created specifically for large retailers and bear their logos. Similarly, many retailers offer holiday buying guides for their customers, normally divided by price point. Appearing in these guides also requires negotiated payment and should be judged on an experience basis.

PROMOTION OF THE PRODUCT THROUGH COOPERATIVE ADVERTISING

Retailers, both large and small, purchase newspaper, radio, and television commercials. Traditions across retailing provide for "coop" advertising. Under these plans, typically, the manufacturer absorbs a certain portion of the price of an ad (usually 50 percent) up to a maximum amount based on a percentage of sales. An example might be that a manufacturer will pay up to 50 percent of the cost of an ad, to the extent that it promotes their product, up to 3 percent of yearly gross purchases. If an ad's content is only 25 percent of the total space, the coop portion is half of the 25 percent devoted to the customer's product.

PROMOTION OF THE PRODUCT DIRECTLY TO STORE PERSONNEL

Many wholesalers and retailers have periodic meetings for their store managers to allow them to become familiar with their product line. Floor salespersons in computer, electronics, and office superstores are an important source of information and can make a sale based on their recommendation to customers. Of all the types of promotion that are in common use, this may be the most neglected.

The most important person in the world is a customer in a store with an interest in buying. Anything that improves your chances of making the sale goes directly to your bottom line.

LIMITED-TIME SPECIAL PROMOTIONS

Among the most critical sources of profits and volume are "promotions" at retailers. Promotions are special, limited-time displays of goods, usually at a promotional (reduced) price. In many cases, promotions are in special-purpose displays. Promotions are partially a response to difficulties that are encountered with stocking and restocking products.

A special-purpose fixture, like a corrugated display or temporary rack, is correctly stocked when it first goes out. Promotional fixtures can combine all the possible point of sale promotions, including rebates, special pricing, signage, and publication.

Given our brief course in the basic terms of sale and the issues to negotiate when making a retail sale, we can now consider each of the subchannels.

TRADITIONAL WHOLESALE

Under this arrangement, the manufacturer sells large bulk quantities to the wholesaler. The wholesaler then sells to retailers and assumes responsibility for payment. Obviously, the wholesaler will demand a discount larger than that which the manufacturer would give to retailers. This is because the manufacturer must sell the product with sufficient margin to make a profit for the wholesaler, but not increase the price too highly, so that the wholesaler cannot come close to meeting the manufacturer's direct price.

The typical discount given to a wholesaler varies from 30 to 40 percent off the MSRP. Payment terms range from thirty to ninety days. An additional allowance may be made for marketing, development, or advertising. These allowances will vary from 1 to 4 percent. For a major campaign such as participation in national television commercials, significant additional sums will be negotiated.

An ideal relationship between a manufacturer and wholesaler would be a cooperative teaming approach, in which the wholesaler takes some responsibility for promoting the goods and securing preferred shelf space. The reengineering and total quality movements suggest a new type of commitment between suppliers and vendors to increase quality and to simplify distribution.

Where the concept of traditional wholesale in regard to computer programs breaks down is that software is almost always sold with a return privilege. Therefore, the manufacturer is in almost the same situation when selling to a retailer as to a wholesaler, but at a lower price. Since the wholesaler is autonomously selling product, it may make poor choices that may generate returns. This implies that a manufacturer would be better off dealing directly with retailers. A countervailing idea is that because wholesalers and retailers usually have significant relationships, the wholesaler may be more able to manage returns or get additional time for product to stay on the shelves. So the difference in price can be made up by lower returns.

Another reason that both a manufacturer and retailer may prefer the intermediary of a wholesaler is capital. If the wholesaler's capital is used, it lessens the amount of capital that the manufacturer must have to fill orders. Sometimes retailers purchase from the wholesaler because the wholesaler provides better credit terms to the retailer than a manufacturer can. Theoretically, the wholesaler also provides services to the retailer beyond credit, like technical assistance from their sales department and warehousing.

Manufacturers do not want to sell direct to small accounts because of all the logistical problems involved. In order to fill a relatively small order, the manufacturer has a paperwork burden for credit and fulfillment, equivalent to filling a large order. This makes the smaller order unprofitable for the manufacturer. Certain wholesalers specialize in selling small quantities of goods to small accounts, including part-time VARs working out of their garages.

However, many retailers prefer, for logistical reasons, to limit the number of vendors with whom they do business and may have minimum-dollar targets to qualify a supplier to go direct. These are usually in the range of $500,000 to $1 million.

A retailer may prefer a wholesaler because of financial stability. If the product does not sell through, will an unknown company be in business in the event that goods must be returned? A wholesaler is more likely to be there to settle up. Most returns, marketing development funds, and slotting fees are deducted from invoices. If a product fails, and no sums are due from the retailer on a particular product, the retailer is in the position of having to collect from the manufacturer. On a single-product company that doesn't have a track record of success, the credibility of a wholesaler may be a significant factor in giving the program retail shelf space. In this case, the wholesaler is doing a significant service to the developer.

In late 1995 and again in the beginning of 1996, a number of companies that had single hit titles were encouraged by retailers to make more titles, on the theory that if the company programmed one winner, it will create new ones. Insiders at the time were concerned about the risks of "brand extension," and later in the release cycle, several of the companies that had programmed one winner left the software business entirely because of losses incurred by the new projects.

On the other hand, if there is an intermediary who is at risk for returns, product can end up in locations that the manufacturer would not normally want to take on a return basis. All the reengineering principles strongly favor a cooperative, long-term approach to vendor–supplier relationships. It should be everyone's goal, regardless of the intermediaries, to have direct contact with customers to accommodate legitimate mutually beneficial goals.

MANUFACTURER DIRECT

You might expect that manufacturer direct is the dominant means by which goods arrive in the retail channel. In fact, although significant, it is not the dominant mode of distribution. Although the developer would prefer manufacturer direct relationships, it is normally retailers who insist on the intermediary. The typical discount is 50 percent plus 10 percent or more (or 55 percent, but there is a tradition of quoting prices in that manner). Slotting fees range from $40 to $300 per facing per store. Payment terms vary from 2 percent ten days, net thirty to sixty days.

DUMP BIN AND DISTRESSED MERCHANDISE

A new, very profitable niche has appeared in the computer software sales industry, special sales through dedicated promotions in "dump bins," usually of "oldenware." A dump bin is a, usually cardboard, box, displayed in an end cap or other desirable location.

Oldenware is software that sold well at one time but is technologically obsolete. Normally, oldenware titles are sold for one-fourth to one-third of their original retail price.

The merchandise is not old inventory, but new inventory specifically manufactured for the purpose of making one more stab at the market with a concept that has some vitality left. Oldenware distribution is quite profitable. It looks like a great deal to the customer since they see programs that are known to them to have been on the market for $59 to $99, but are now at $14.95 or less. Typical discounts are 60 percent off retail. Normally, slotting fees are absorbed by the distributor.

RACK JOBBERS

Rack jobbing was created in response to the sudden appearance of a lucrative, but maddening, market: top 45-rpm records. Millions and millions of dollars worth of "singles" were consumed by teenagers, but, picking what was hot and then managing the fad was too much for retailers used to having a full season to shift between summer and winter clothes. Do you purchase and sell a few thousand more Elvis singles, or is the latest release from the Beatles better? Retailers faced either adding more home office employees charged with buying hit records and committing substantial sums of money on guessing the latest fad or getting out of the record business.

Rack jobbers entered the void by offering to manage inventory for retailers. Rack jobbers offered a form of partnership and risk sharing. Under a rack jobbing arrangement, the rack jobber takes inventory regularly and takes responsibility for balancing the inventory. The retailer pays only for merchandise that is sold.

The arrangement reduced one risk but came with another risk for the retailer. Both the record company and the retailer gave the rack jobber extra discounts and additional payment, respectively. This relationship requires significant trust on both sides. The rack jobber is at risk and can limit its exposure by stocking low amounts of everything, hits or misses. So can the retailer be sure that it is earning as much as possible? Rack jobbing required a great deal of trust among the parties to the arrangement.

With a rack jobbing arrangement, can the record producer be sure that it is also selling enough product? The problem with returns is again created for the party creating the records. The rack jobbing industry also created the "cut out," old inventory marked by notching the album cover and sold at a low price.

A variation on rack jobbing was to lease the entire record area to a specialist in the music industry. The lessee, usually with its own dedicated cash registers, paid a set fee for the right to occupy the space in the store and normally contributed to advertising and overhead. Some of the arrangements also included revenue sharing between the lessee and the retailer. Over time, as the hit record business became better understood, the number of leased departments dropped, as did rack jobbing.

When industry insiders meet and talk about rack jobbing or leased departments, they are usually thought of as "escape strategies." Merchants who feel that they can't afford to be out of a particular business, like hit records, but aren't sure that they can make a profit or are not committed to the area, lease the department or put the responsibility of the department on rack jobbers or concessionaires. Rack jobbing or laying off the responsibility on another tends to reduce profit since the rack jobber has to charge more for the goods than through other arrangements. Retail executives don't emphasize or champion low-profit problematic areas.

When prerecorded videotape entered the market, the rack jobbing industry was revitalized since it was a new commodity with which retailers had no experience. It was déjà vu for retailers. They now faced something else that they didn't understand and couldn't realistically stock for themselves. Rack jobbing enjoyed a renaissance in supplying the public with prerecorded videotape and handling stocking and returns for the retailers.

Rack jobbing remains a part of the computer market and, in particular, for retail outlets with little experience in selling software. Discounts are slightly higher than for retail sales. Payment terms are from sixty to ninety days.

NONTRADITIONAL RETAILERS

These include electronic distributors, school distributors, and nontraditional distributors.

Electronic distributors

Traditional computer bulletin board systems (BBSs) were always capable of acting as online stores. Many different software programs were available for BBS sysops to sell anything. Although security was a concern, BBS connections were almost always direct phone calls without any relays, resulting in confidence that so long as the telephone call was secure, the transaction was secure. A small amount of commerce was engaged in over BBSs that were relatively small. Most sales were for software created by the owner of the BBS. Few third-party sales were made.

The Internet presents an entirely different series of security problems. Your calls may be routed through multiple networks and are often bounced all over the world. The Internet is excellent at the free exchange of information, including financial intelligence like credit card numbers. Convincing the public to purchase software through the Internet will require that the buyers are convinced that the transactions are secure.

One other factor may limit electronic software sales over the Internet. Almost all software sales made electronically are made because the purchaser wants immediate delivery of the program, through either downloading the program or using an unlock key. People don't want to order goods over the net for mail order. That's easier via fax or phone, and consumers do not adopt technology unless it is convenient to them. Programs are becoming significantly larger, and have suddenly increased because of the shift to CD distribution.

Even with compression and a fast Internet line, sending a 20- to 30-megabyte program becomes an ordeal of hours. This nascent market is entirely different from any others. Unless physical goods are also delivered, the cost structure is entirely different. After all, there are physical production costs for electronically delivered software. There are no "typical" terms for this industry.

School distributors

The academic market is served by a series of distributors familiar with servicing the unique needs of schools. Schools tend to place orders for various programs and site licenses up for competitive bidding. Qualifying to bid requires significant paperwork burdens. In addition, schools have special credit terms that require setting up banking or other arrangements to carry receivables.

Selling to schools requires a special mindset. Instructors and curriculum designers ask school distributors to locate programs for their courses, often requiring extensive work by the distributor. A school distributor will locate a program that is perfect for a particular course, demonstrate the program, and then find that the purchasing department places the order out for competitive bids. Having done all the work, a distributor can lose an order. Typical terms are structured so that the distributor can earn approximately 20 percent of retail while preserving a discount for the school.

Nontraditional distributors

Nontraditional distributors fall into two categories. The first is existing businesses that are broadening their lines to include software. The other is startup concepts in the distribution of software.

Some of the existing businesses that are now broadening into software include magazine and news dealers and traditional book publishers. Magazine readership has declined over recent years, yet the number of magazines being started continues unabated. Strenuous efforts have been made by the magazine industry to increase readership with limited success. As a result, in order to keep volume growing, news agents that rack job magazine and newspapers have now added software into their mixes. The results to date have been mixed, with few distributors making big hits. However, these companies have not discovered some of the secrets of impulse merchandising of software.

Some new businesses have appeared that are banking on software being a commodity item, and they are looking to distribute in places that have no or at best very limited experience in software, such as drug stores or groceries.

Given your introduction to retail, the next logical question is how to get in the door. For those without industry contacts, the best bet is to get an industry insider on your side — a series of manufacturers' representatives. Good representatives are well connected and can get your program's concept a realistic hearing before buyers. The best representatives limit themselves to a region, but work it very well.

Developers should consider a number of issues when negotiating the finer points of contracts for retail distribution:

- Payment terms may be illusory. Unfortunately, there is an industrywide suspicion among developers that many accounts consider the payment terms negotiated as the beginnings of further renegotiation. It is generally not a good idea to offer discounts for prompt payment although some accounts are known for being extremely prompt in payment. Many accounts will pay the discounted price even when they are paying late rather than early.

- Reorders are where the money is made. The initial order is great. However, it is vital to obtain sell through information from retailers so that you can take steps to get a new order or to get the product moving. Be sure to have your contracts require that you receive sell through information as quickly as possible. Almost all retailers have computerized inventory control and can provide detailed sell through information. Without sell through information, you are selling blind.

A sample retail contract is shown in Appendix 1.

CHAPTER 6

▷ OEM Distribution

Software entrepreneurs can meet the goal of selling a million copies of their software in two ways. The first is to sell a million copies to a million different customers directly, whether at retail or by direct marketing. You present your program, in your packaging, to users who purchase single copies of the software.

The second way is to sell software bundled in other firms' products. By making one sale, you potentially authorize thousands of resales. Fortunately, these two roads are not exclusive; they are, in fact, complementary. Is OEM (original equipment manufacturing) software licensing a good business? The fortunes of the preeminent software company in the world, Microsoft, rest on OEM distribution of operating systems. OEM distribution, also called bundling, is a market channel in which software is combined with computer hardware, peripherals, or other software at a single price. OEM bundling is a great form of advertising and an excellent way to build brand awareness.

OEM distribution may be the best of all possible worlds for software entrepreneurs. In addition to wide distribution and public awareness revenue from OEM sales, as a supplier of OEM software your company can build a loyal customer base, which will provide a long-term revenue stream for many upgrades and new versions of your software.

OEM sales truly substitute creativity and intellectual capital for money. In almost all cases of OEM marketing of software, the developer gives a single copy of the software and manual to the OEM. The OEM bears all the costs of replication, packaging, and distribution. The developer gains entry into the market together with advertising of the best kind — your software is on the user's machine. With clever sales work, a large number of sales are made with an absolute minimum commitment in inventory and distribution costs. Can't afford slotting fees, returns, market development funds (MDFs) and don't have the financial strength to carry receivables for sixty to ninety days? Only OEM bundling combines large guaranteed distribution with low investment.

There are several different kinds of OEM bundling. The most familiar of these includes software with a complete system or peripheral. Recently, the Internet has created bundling opportunities in which service providers package software with their service. Software developers with CD-ROMs to fill are now bundling software within their software. As the software market matures toward becoming a commodity item, a new OEM channel of "store branded" software is slowly emerging as a viable channel. Software is becoming universal enough that bundling opportunities in noncomputer products are starting to appear.

Every computer peripheral requires drivers to interact with the computer. As a result, most bundling occurs more often in the context of hardware or peripheral sales rather than with software. All the peripheral hardware installed on your computer uses "drivers," special software programs that handle the interaction of that peripheral with your computer. Because every piece of hardware needs a software driver, most bundled software is packaged with peripheral components, rather than with other software. A "better" driver is always available, whether or not your operating system's default driver works; besides which, the drivers shipped on "plug-and-play" PCs can become obsolete overnight, and unable to support the latest features of your new peripheral. In many cases, the hardware manufacturers create "superdrivers" that provide much more than just the interface between the system and the peripheral. These include extensive extra utilities, visual status screens, or error-trapping routines. OEM software can be regular drivers, superdrivers, or software not directly related to operating the peripheral.

OEM software is an entrée to huge numbers of consumers. OEM bundling is a form of advertising, except that you are paid rather than having to pay for advertising. Like being on the shelf with commercial products marketed under your name, being bundled in other products is referential advertising. As an OEM, the goal is to develop a two-way stream of revenue: whatever can be gained for the initial price for bundling, and then further revenue from selling upgrades or updates to the existing customers. OEM software, so long as you capture the names of your users, creates a valuable mailing list. A typical plan for maximum financial return from OEM placement by getting a high rate of registrations is to:

- Rent customer names and addresses as mailing lists.

- Offer immediate upgrades to a version of the OEM software containing more features.

- Market new versions of the software to the installed user base.

- Offer other software you create to the customers.

Market forces will encourage anyone making a CD for any reason to fill it as full as possible. In the field of disk sales of shareware, the market began with disks holding just a few programs, and ultimately changed to filling disks as full as possible. After all, the customer realizes that the cost is the same whether the CD is full or empty.

Getting the thousands, hundreds of thousands, or millions of persons who receive your software in another package to install it and then to register is a difficult marketing job. Unless you contact your customers to inform them of upgrades and updates, they are unlikely to know about them. You are asking a customer to take the time to fill out a card or to run a registration form routine in your program. Your user would much rather just use his or her new computer or computer accessory. Since the ultimate value of bundling is building a customer base, when negotiating an OEM sales agreement, negotiate for access to the OEM's own mailing list to obtain the names of users registering the product package in which your software is bundled.

The best designed OEM bundling registration schemes have return rates of 5 to 10 percent. Among those companies willing to divulge registration rates, the normal reported rates for companies that do *not* pay postage range from 1 to 5 percent, whereas those that pay postage range from 5 to 10 percent. Those using automatic fax or e-mail registration in addition to mailed-in materials have slightly higher registration rates.

An additional profit center for bundling deals is developing a mailing list. Mailing lists of purchasers of computer programs are a valuable commodity.

They are "rented" to a hungry market of direct mail merchants who want to mail to prospects that are known to have bought items that correlate well to their product. Names are most valuable right after a sale. A higher price is paid for the names of persons who have purchased in the last ninety days. Although you can rent your mailing list yourself, a good mailing list broker will get more revenue. Brokers require that a mailing list contain a minimum of five thousand names before they will accept the list for marketing. Since you must approve all rentals of your mailing list, you do not have a risk of renting your list to a competitor. Rental rates vary from $25 per thousand to five or six times that for the most recent and high-value respondents.

The most successful companies encourage registration by the following strategies:

- Additional support in exchange for registration

- Contests for persons who register

- Guaranteed free upgrade to the next version of the software

- Web or fax registration

- Lock outs

- Lock ins

ADDITIONAL SUPPORT IN EXCHANGE FOR REGISTRATION

Although it is the most commonly used strategy to get registrations, it is also the worst incentive. If your program works superbly and has great online documentation, why should the user take the time to register? Customers like the idea of the availability of support, but all customers would prefer never needing to use the help desk. As online help has become better, OEM like all other software relies less on printed documentation, and more on context-sensitive help and hypertext help documents. Online documentation is favored because it can be longer, more detailed, and even feature video. Use of online documentation eliminates the cost of printing. You should capture the name of those calling for support — but don't rely on this as a source of registrations.

CONTESTS FOR PERSONS WHO REGISTER

This is an excellent strategy if the contest is a good fit to the program. Using a carrot makes more sense than using the stick of "no support" without registering. Be sure that your prize is something that is worth your customer's time and investment of a first-class stamp. A trivial or unattractive prize won't motivate. Companies with $10 million contests don't get a 100 percent return. If your contest is for low-value prizes, it will not significantly add to your registration rate. One other hint: do the drawing weekly or monthly; the more often that you have the contest drawings, the more likely that the person will register.

GUARANTEED FREE UPGRADE TO THE NEXT VERSION
OF THE SOFTWARE

This is a very good idea. Starting in 1994 and mid-1995, software developers found that persons didn't buy software pending the often delayed release of Windows 95. To impart motion to a buying public insisting on inertia, the "risk" of obsolescence is removed by offering a free upgrade to the next version. As electronic distribution of software becomes more common, the cost to the developer for offering new versions shrinks. This is especially promising as the best way to get registrations because the lucky coincidence is that many users prefer the immediate gratification of getting software from a BBS or the Internet. Having an e-mail address is just as good as a street address since solicitations for new programs is easier on the Internet than by mail.

WEB OR FAX REGISTRATION

Electronic registration is a convenience to users with modems and a very practical use of the Internet. Electronic registration removes the issue of postage from the user's decision, and by experienced users is quite likely to be used. Using electronic registration on the Internet also has the desirable side effect of introducing persons to your web page. If they like what they see, the customer will return to your web page to learn about the latest developments at your company.

LOCK OUTS

Some developers code in a routine that does not permit the user to use the program without entering an unlock code. This gathers names of users since the only way to get an unlock code is by calling or mailing in the registration information. The lock out can occur before the software is "activated" or after a certain number of days or uses. Although the rate of compliance will be high among those using the software, the rate of snapping the disks or CDs in half may be higher, and the rate of future sales will be low. Lock outs are defended by their proponents with religious fervor. In my own dealings, I have met developers who make their living on upgrades or updates who take an unreasoning posture of using coercion. Others try it and fail, and then follow conventional wisdom and try something else.

LOCK INS

This is the opposite of a lock out. When the user registers, he or she gets an unlock code that allows access to more features or perhaps another program. If for some reason you lock out a feature that a user wants to use right away, you may irritate the user for life. On the other hand, this seems to be a clever, gentle, jujitsu approach of turning a problem into an opportunity.

You can find OEM markets by visiting a large computer superstore. The following hardware generally have these OEM bundles:

- Printers — clip art, "light" desktop publishers, greeting card generators

- Mice, pointing devices — mouse "radar," games

- CD-ROM readers — samplers of any kind, multimedia recording software

- Monitors — screen savers, photo samplers, illustration programs

- Modems — Internet browsers, terminal programs, online games, fax software

- Joy sticks and other game controllers — games, online games

- Scanners — OCR software

All software titles delivered on CD-ROM are potential targets for OEM sales provided that the CD can hold the program.

Computers and most peripherals must be sold with some bundled software. Customers rightfully demand that a new computer, an investment of $1,500 or more, have operating system software and utilities. However, almost every piece of hardware requires software before it can be used at all, and marketing concerns have made bundling software essential. As prices of different computer hardware items come closer and closer together as the "commoditization" of computer hardware continues, one of the only ways to differentiate peripherals is through brand names or software bundles.

At the same time that customers want software bundled in transactions of $1,500 or more, lower-end customers are even more demanding in insisting on getting software with the machine. As the computer industry continues its struggle to market a $500 system, the need for manufacturers to have good software bundles increases. The $1,500 or more computer system purchaser may resist additional investments in software or peripherals, but the $500 purchaser may be unable to absorb further transactional costs. Ultra low-cost bundles for super high-volume distribution will become vitally important if this market is to be tapped.

Manufacturers of computers also provide software with their machines in self-defense — by preloading the proper drivers and operating system software, manufacturers avoid thousands of hours of support calls.

Within the very early history of microcomputer sales, independent VARs and SIs (systems integrators) provided additional software and systems programming for their customers. This usually involved changing the system bootup to invoke a menu program that provided shortcuts to the applications the customer wanted to run. The bad part of this "service" was that many menu programs didn't have any provision for adding new programs, or for exiting the menu completely.

Preloaded software was a significant marketing tool for selling computers at retail until software program interchangeability became an issue to software users. Second, preloaded software was acceptable to users before there was brand awareness of specific programs. Early microcomputer users were thrilled to have any word processor at all when their computers cost $3,000 or more and no word processor had any significant awareness among consumers.

Returning to the present market, the margins earned by retailers on sales of computers have been stagnant or even declining. Prices for machines tend to be very close whether at retail or through mail order. "Extras," most especially software bundles, become the most important means of differentiating peripherals other than brand name awareness.

A new model of computer purchaser dominates the industry. Experts peg PC penetration in 35 percent of American homes. Most of the machines being sold are to those who already own them; that is, the same persons are upgrading their systems rather than new persons buying machines. To broaden the market share, new computers would have to appeal to computer-phobic persons.

The first-time buyer is intimidated by the hidden costs after the investment in a machine. For example, for $1,500 or so, they get a machine, but no printer. The printer costs extra, and so does the cable for the printer. This goes on and on since every application area needs further investments in peripherals and the like. By bundling software, the sales staff has a much easier job.

To obtain OEM bundling deals, you can act as your own sales force. Create a list of affinity programs or peripherals that are related to your program, and then use industry guides to locate prospects. Many OEM deals are struck at the major trade shows like Comdex, E3, and Consumer Electronics Show. Some OEMs rely on agents to make OEM placements.

The future of OEM bundling looks very bright. Older machines are being replaced with new machines that have CD players. As new-generation CDs, which will hold more data, are released, CDs will become the dominant way that software is distributed. Besides the efficiency of CDs for distributing large programs, customers will demand larger and faster CDs because their ability to offer higher-quality video will ensure that the public upgrades or buys machines with better mass storage devices.

CDs now hold about 650 megabytes of data in PC format, but new technologies will increase this many times. If the growth curve is at all similar to that of floppy disks, which grew from 180 kilobytes to 2.88 megabytes, and now feature 20 megabytes or more in a more expensive format, CDs will increase the amount of data fifty to a hundred times. The cost of duplicating a CD in quantity will also drop. At present market prices, a price of 40 cents to 50 cents per CD prevails in larger runs. With further efficiencies, it will be possible for peripherals costing only a few dollars to have a CD bundled. The lowest cost mice and other peripherals have retail prices below $9. The manufacturers of these types of goods must limit their bundled software to a single disk, since they must keep their production costs as low as possible. Unlike CDs which presently cost 40–50 cents per copy, disks can be purchased for 17 to 23 cents each.

Be sure to be extremely vigilant in planning the extent of support that you offer. Support usually is thought of as an expense to control. For an OEM bundling arrangement, support *is* your sales department. Your support desk must not only help users, but it must also sell the software. It is your life blood and requires that your sales personnel convert help desk inquiries to sales.

Telephone companies can provide you with reports showing the number of calls and busy signals to your support telephone numbers. If these reports show an excessive number of calls are not completed, there are firms that will accept transfers of incoming calls and handle support for a fee.

Too many bundling sales opportunities are lost because of unrealistic pricing demands by software owners. Any revenue from bundling is found money and an opportunity to build a loyal customer base. Pricing for bundles is constrained by two factors. Your price must be a small enough percentage to the overall wholesale costs of the OEM product that the cost of your software does not force a significant change in the wholesale price point. The total price for bundling is also constrained by the fact that if you demand too much, it will be cheaper for the OEM to create its own program.

If an OEM agrees to license your software for $1 per copy, the OEM will mark that up to the wholesaler, and the retailer then marks up the item again. One dollar added into the cost of product raises the retail street price $3 to $4 because of the multiple layers of markup. For example, a mouse with a street price of $30 would have to have its retail price increased to $34 to cover the addition of a $1 utility. An 11.33 percent price increase will be a significant change in position for a $30 product. To make realistic pricing decisions for OEM bundles, the parties must work together and share information on costs of production and the effect to the retail customer of the addition of the cost of the OEM bundle to make the OEM program successful.

In an ultra high-volume bundling transaction, even a trivial cost per program duplicated can equal the price of having the program written. For example, a desktop publishing utility bundled with a half million printers will cost $250,000 at 50 cents a copy. A printer distributor can get a very nice program developed for $50,000 and own it outright.

Although the fee for the OEM bundling must represent a profit center for the software developer, the price must be discounted by the fact that the software developer is being given advantage of the OEM's capital and marketing investment, and is building a customer base. In order to make a bundling deal that both sides can be happy with, the primary focus for the software provider should not be on the price per unit, but on developing a long-term relationship. For example, an OEM may be willing to absorb some of the cost of the software bundle if it can make up the loss of margin in increased sales.

Some developers treat OEM as a one-shot deal and license software with unlimited reproduction for a one-time charge. In these types of OEM arrangements, there are no upgrades or bouncebacks. This can be a profitable business, but it is usually limited to drivers that are bundled with $9 retail mice, or blank carton, generic video cards. However, since the lowest cost peripherals (like $9 mice) need to pay the lowest possible price for software and packaging, the absolute amount that you can make is less than if you'd been bundled with more expensive hardware. Accordingly, solely targeting this market will severely limit overall profitability, particularly since there will be no upgrade potential. There is no reason not to do both, however, and have one version of the software for high-quality bundles, and another for the one-time fee market, and sell both. Given the investment in creating a program, there's no reason to pass up the additional income of one-time bundles. Since $10 programs and $100 programs are different channels, ultra low-cost mice and peripherals are a different channel from higher-priced, brand name components.

The more important clauses to points to negotiate are:

- Length of agreement. The program provider must, in exchange for agreeing to a price that makes sense for the OEM manufacturer, get a very long commitment. If a software developer will commit to making the investment necessary to develop an excellent add-on for the program, and then to make new versions of the add-ons as operating systems or market conditions change, the OEM should agree to a long-term commitment to the developer.

- Sharing of registered user's names. The OEM and developer should share lists of users who register so that both have access to the information for building their respective user mailing lists.

- Options on other bundles. The developer should request an option, or right of first refusal, to create any other software that may be bundled with the OEM product.

- Access to marketing data. Given a confidentiality agreement, the OEM should provide an outline of marketing information, including the identities of wholesale and retail outlets, wholesale and retail prices, and sell through. This information is necessary for the developer to plan customer support and to measure registration and upsale performance.

- Access to OEM's plans. Again, given a confidentiality agreement between the parties, the OEM should advise the developer of marketing goals and promotions in advance to allow the developer to plan support staffing requirements.

Appendix 8 contains an OEM agreement incorporating the provisions described here.

CHAPTER 7

▷ Government and Corporate Sales

Developers' first targets for high-volume software sales usually don't include the federal government. Although the government is cutting "growth," government sales are nevertheless a viable channel. When the headlines read "government budget cuts," it may be the best time to start selling, since the easily discouraged will give up and look elsewhere for business.

Corporate and other large organizations purchase several billion dollars of software yearly. Unlike the government, corporate investment in software is guaranteed to increase in the foreseeable future. This is a key market, and as we will discuss, the institutional market has significant financial advantages over retail sales.

In budget battles, there are winners and losers. Given that the government appears to be mired in management-by-crisis mode, Peter will be robbed to pay Paul. After all, the best way to give the appearance of doing *something* is to announce funding shifts in favor of the "problème de jour." My personal experience supports the cynical conclusion that some organizations always will have too much money and others not enough. At this time, educational institutions, prisons, and the military have the capacity to purchase large amounts of software.

Remember that the U.S. government is the largest purchaser of goods and services, ever. Experts estimate that out of $200 billion in goods and services purchased by the government, $40 billion is purchased from small business. This is a marketplace that can quickly buy large numbers of copies of your software.

A "reality check" about the government's procurement policies is in order. Whatever you may have heard about $700 toilets, the government's contracting officers work for a low price. If you review actual contract awards, you will find that for contracts on standard items (or items that have equivalents on the open market), the government will get a price significantly lower than high-unit wholesalers pay for the same quantity. This is because there is no credit risk in selling to the government and the contracts are stable, normally for relatively long terms. In any regular sale, the seller must factor in both the time value of their money and the inevitable delay. "Inevitable delay" refers to the fact that with few exceptions most businesses purchasing software, whether retailers or wholesalers, consider payment terms to be nominal. There are always delays, deductions, and complaints in sales, except to the government.

There are other reasons the government often gets a lower initial price. The larger the quantity, the lower the price. As the largest volume purchaser in the world, the government can use the tremendous volume of its purchases for leverage in lowering the price. The government also enters into contracts over a longer period than most other parties. Some companies view government procurement as stable, low-profit-margin work, which they use to reduce incremental costs of all production. If the government purchases large quantities of goods, larger quantities of materials are purchased overall, increasing the profit margin on regular sales at quantity discounts on larger supplies.

Selling software to any government agency or institution has special challenges. The corporate world usually lags behind consumers in upgrading to more powerful computer hardware. Institutional users use hardware longer than the general public since the cost to upgrade is a multimillion-dollar decision.

Government agencies lag significantly behind for-profit corporations in the power of their hardware. Nevertheless, the successful mass market entrepreneur views this as a challenge rather than an obstacle. How do you make high-volume sales to target users with old, limited-capability hardware?

First, you can create two versions of your software: one that you will offer to consumers and their target hardware and one that is limited in capability specifically for the government and older hardware market. Or if your government purchaser has adequate budget funding available, you can bundle and sell hardware, or upgrades to existing hardware, with your software.

Since the government and institutions have unique concerns, you should consider renaming your software specifically for government sales. Institutions and the government characteristically also respond well to the bundling of training in the use of software specifically for their vertical market use of your broad-based software. Whatever your program, understanding the specific use that the government agency will make of it is vital to closing the sale.

Fortunately, the information is easy to obtain. Institutions have standard forms to fill, standardized reports to complete, and specific types of data to crunch. Contracting officers and in-house programmers are usually willing to make their needs known.

Insiders who have played the government and institutional sales contracting gambit have secured a great deal of their intelligence at trade shows and professional meetings. You will find many in-house programmers and computer administrators attending large shows like Comdex or E3. They will be both end users and administrators. Each will have a "wish list," and if your software matches their lists, you have a target to pursue.

The federal government, as a policy matter, gives preference to "small businesses" in procurement. An abstruse series of regulations with the deceptively simple title of Federal Acquisition Regulations (FARs) cover the government's purchasing. The FARs define what a small business is for each SIC (Standard Industrial Code). "Prepackaged software" businesses, category 7373, has a limit of $7 million in annual revenue. "Small" is obviously a relative term; $7 million in revenue is considered "small" for the purposes of qualifying for the small business set-aside.

Historically, the government doesn't meet its small business set-aside target. Some agencies take the statutory direction seriously and actively seek out small business vendors. Others view the goal as another paperwork and administrative hassle. The branches of the military are among the most open to purchasing from small businesses.

The traditional approach for selling to the government is to work closely with the Small Business Administration. The SBA has programs in place to assist small businesses. However, the SBA programs are geared toward traditional procurement of stock items and services. That means bidding on standard commodities and services in competitive bidding. Your goal is different: you want to sell *your* software to the government.

The FARs provide that a company may present an unsolicited contract proposal (UCP) to any government agency. If you are a small business entity, you receive preferential treatment when you present a UCP. If everything works according to the rules, if you present a UCP with any merit and are a small business entity, the agency is supposed to work with you, the proponent of the proposal, to award a contract. The concept is, instead of trying to bid for work on government specifications, you have the government take your goods as they are, on your negotiated terms.

Making unsolicited proposals is governed by subpart 15.5 of the FARs. (The complete regulations are in Appendix 3.) In ordinary, competitive bidding acquisitions, contact with the contracting officer is severely limited. However, the FARs strongly suggest that the proponent of the unsolicited proposal discuss the government's interests in the offer with the purchasing officer.

Unsolicited contract proposals are not limited to traditional sales. A UCP can also request that the government evaluate or test software provided at low cost or no cost. Why would you do that? Getting a glowing government recommendation for your software can be the basis of a sales campaign, and a trial is an excellent way to "get your foot in the door."

This book has many messages. One of them is that brains can substitute for capital in the software business. Getting a UCP to promote sales of your software is one of the best examples of using intellectual ability to gain business rather than capital. Your UCP could request that the government use your software to see if it improves the efficiency or capabilities of the agency. Upon passing the "test," the software may then be adopted as an official standard or recommended standard.

To submit a UCP that will be accepted, you must tie your proposal to the mission statement of the agency. Every agency must make a yearly mission statement. Mission statements are taken very seriously as the basic directions for operation of the agency. In drafting your UCP, include clear references to how your product will help the agency meet its mission.

Appendix 2 contains the complete mission statement of the Library of Congress, an organization that consumes a great deal of computer software. We will use its mission statement as an example for preparing a UCP.

The mission statement of the Library of Congress provides us with several uses for off-the-shelf software with only minor changes. The first and second priorities are closely related, in that the Library plans to create a universal collection of human knowledge. Accordingly, a UCP that proposes a means to collect knowledge automatically and make it available to others would fit the agency mission. Dozens of companies are creating Internet browsers and Internet information retrieval and cataloging programs. A great UCP might be an intelligent ferret browser that continuously goes through the Internet collecting, cataloging, and comparing newsgroup articles.

The heart of the unsolicited proposal is the technical abstract. UCPs must contain a two-hundred-word abstract describing the products and services to be provided to the government. The ideal UCP has been molded by discussions with the contracting officers and end users, and ties in to the mission statement. The abstract, like a query letter, must be a carefully honed presentation of the compelling reasons to do the project. Like busy publishing directors, upper-level government executives must approve substantial contract commitments in short periods (for example, before the end of the fiscal year). You may remember a recent governmental scandal in which a report was changed before presentation. The body of the report was kept the same. Only the executive summary and conclusions were changed so that they were totally different from the original report. Put energy in that summary and abstract!

A few entrepreneurs have succeeded in using government agencies as a source of venture capital for initial program development. There are a few variations on this theme. The first is to obtain a contract for development of a program at cost for a government agency, but retaining rights for sales of the program as is, or in different versions, to others. In this way, the government can obtain custom software at cost, and the developer gets funding to develop the software, and then can resell the software, typically to other governments and government contractors.

In developing software for institutional users, keep in mind that large institutions have unique concerns. Some of these concerns follow.

INTERNATIONAL SCOPE

Governments and large corporations are located worldwide. Therefore, you need to make provisions for different languages, date format conventions, and currencies. Fortunately, systems software has improved, making some of these modifications simple. The latest editions of RAD software contain drivers for overseas markets. Whatever tasks your program performs, be sensitive for the differences in customary use of commas or periods when writing numbers, and any other differences. As noted in Chapter 3, having your program's strings in separate resource files makes translation a much simpler process.

APPLICATION OF STATUTES REQUIRING "REASONABLE ACCOMMODATION"

The Americans with Disabilities Act and other similar laws require that larger employers and governments make "reasonable accommodations" to allow persons who have physical disabilities to be able to work. Consider how your program would work for those with hearing, sight, or other disabilities. For example, corporate purchasing departments will be impressed if your program has been tested for use by the blind. Virtually every organization must make their workplaces and working tools, like computer programs, accessible by persons with many different types of disabilities.

SECURITY

Whatever your program, governmental and corporate users will be much more concerned with security of data than other users. Every program should be passworded, and data kept encrypted. Security includes the process of making backups. Take the time to include functions in your corporate programs to perform automatic backups, data verification, and record locking. The present dominant operating system, Microsoft Windows, is available in NT specification, which includes record locking and meets military and government standards for security. Consider making changes in your program to specifically provide for working under a high-security environment.

BILLING, LOGGING

Whatever your software does, if there is a way to perform measurements of use, billing, and logging, including job cost tracking, be sure to include these features. Accountability is one of the most important features of modern bureaucracy, and automatic logging of use is vital to business.

ISO QUALITY CERTIFICATION

As noted in Chapter 3, concerning design, ISO quality certification is an internationally recognized mark of quality software development. Obtaining certification under ISO procedures will ease sales to the corporate and government worlds.

LAN, INTRANET, AND INTERNET

Again, even for applications that are traditionally just for single users, providing means for the user to share program data with local area networks (LANs), legacy systems, and "data warehouses" is an important factor in obtaining corporate or governmental acceptance. Fortunately, modern development systems provide open database connectivity (ODBC) drivers and other tools to make this process relatively simple.

REVISION TRACKING

Audit trails are extremely important in the business world. These features are relatively simple to code with modern RAD tools.

DETAILED "SUPPORT" MANUALS AND TRAINING

Most site licenses and government sales require training for in-house management information systems (MIS) personnel. Special-purpose manuals must be created for the institutional use of the program.

Programmers are normally used to selling programs either outright to a user, in the case of customized software, or, at single-copy prices, to retail purchasers. The mistake that loses developers the most deals is overpricing corporate licenses. Computer software executives who are used to retail sales structures generally overprice sales because they consider the number of users as equivalent to retail sales. Generally, governments and corporations are very interested in obtaining well-designed software, but balk at the costs quoted. A completely different pricing strategy is required to sell to governments and large corporations.

Sales made to large customers are entirely different from retail sales. First, there is no slotting fee, no returns, and to their credit, there is a strong possibility of signing up for service contracts and contracts for improved versions. In pricing "corporate" type arrangements, significantly lower levels of support and lower material costs are the typical terms.

Significantly lower levels of support

Corporations and other large-scale users normally provide their own internal support through their in-house MIS departments. Most corporate and governmental users request training for a limited number of key personnel. These key personnel then handle the in-house requests for service. Contracts for corporate sales normally limit support to a limited number of key personnel, who are required to limit their inquiries to issues that represent true bugs. This is a resource rather than a problem since it represents beta testing that is provided free. In developing variations of commercial software for industry, I have also received requests for upgrades or features that were excellent, fresh ideas. Therefore, having good corporate users will also assist your own development efforts.

Lower material costs

In almost every site license agreement, the user acts as a miniature OEM and receives a limited number of disks and manuals and then has in-house personnel install the program. Corporate users are satisfied with one set of disks and manuals per office or location. LANs and intranets often mean that your program will be physically installed on a few servers and then used off and on by many individual computer workstations.

Generally, the price for licenses for more than a thousand users should be priced below the wholesale price of the actual number of copies that are shipped, plus training costs. There is a very practical reason for this recommendation. Institutions can most certainly purchase copies wholesale, and pricing your program above the wholesale price of the copies that they will use encourages them to go to another bidder. As previously noted, sales to institutions are not subject to slotting fees, returns, and MDF charges, so there's room to lower your price accordingly.

There is another very practical tip that you get from veterans of the institutional sales wars. Every institutional contracting officer has a specific dollar limit of authority. If it is within his or her dollar limit, that person can authorize making your deal. One dollar over that amount and another level of approval is required. To make sales more easily, consider the contracting official's authority, and limit the level of reviews the purchase would need. The price received for site licenses is nominal, and almost all of it goes to the bottom line. It is a zero-sum game.

When dealing with institutional purchasers, remember that having your software in large-scale use results in other sales down the road. If your software is adopted, the employees or students may then buy retail copies for their own use. Being familiar with a particular software interface gives you a "captive" market that will probably continue to use your program outside the institution. Contractors dealing with the institution will also purchase software that the institution uses.

A sample description of a corporate sale and pricing is contained in Appendix 6.

Another large government market is the school market. An insider who is on the front lines every day, Pam Ring of Maryland VAR, Software In A Week, is an expert in selling directly to the school market. Her approach consists of integrity and hard work. Although many schools buy whatever is in the two or three catalogs that they get, Ring scours catalogs, stores, and review CDs to make a perfect match for a school's requests.

Ring's requests of software developers are very humbling. She finds that computer programs are not robust, and that in classrooms with thirty computers and one teacher, too many class periods are lost to systems crashing. How do you sell to Ring? Convince her that the program works. This is not an issue of end users not taking the time to learn how to use software. Instead, experienced computer users, well versed in applications, find far too many bugs. To enter the educational market, this insider suggests that there is no substitute for robust software.

Educational software requires many of the same features that were discussed for institutional software. Every title should also have a teacher's guide. Teacher's guides provide suggestions for use of the program in school settings. Example lesson plans are also very useful.

Selling to the educational market is not limited to specifically "educational" titles. General-purpose programs, including all areas of productivity, are needed by schools. The educational market is also one in which the hardware may lag behind that of consumer end users although the situation is slowly improving.

Selling software to educational institutions is done through purchasing space in catalogs as well as by making your software known to educators and VARs who serve local schools. Pricing for schools also has traditions. Schools generally purchase "packs," or school districtwide licenses. Typical pricing would address five, ten, or thirty packs of the program. These prices should again be somewhat less than normal wholesale.

Many school districts request licenses for districtwide use. These unlimited licenses are among the most profitable types of sales. Pricing is a matter of negotiation, but it's "found money." Making districtwide sales has the same trickle-down effect in the retail market as other large institutional sales.

Since the consumer marketplace is more or less stagnant, with the penetration of computers frozen at about 30 percent of households, the institutional market will become one of the few areas where growth will occur. Developers will have to make significant commitments to these market channels to reach high-volume sales.

CHAPTER 8

▷ The Internet and Software Sales

The Internet is now the hottest topic in the computer field. Every computer software developer has a plan for dealing with the net, believing it represents a potential mass marketing force in its own right. But is the net's potential worthy of the hype? In this chapter, I discuss whether the hype is deserved. The basic questions that computer software developers need answers to are:

1. How large is the Internet now, and what is the potential for growth?

2. What types of programs have the potential to become big winners in the marketplace?

3. What direct effect will the Internet have on traditional retailing of computer software?

The growth of the Internet has been a shock to computer industry insiders. The corporate world has been very slow to adopt the net, and until late 1996, many government and business leaders were asking their technical staff or outside consultants whether the net was "real" and here to stay. A brief history lesson about the net is vital to understanding why many persons have been "gun shy" of the Internet.

The principal reason that many persons are shocked about the net is that no one saw it coming. ARPANET and DARPANET, the precursors of the net, as well as BBSs, were curiosities until just a few years ago. If someone used conventional BBSs or the net before 1994, it was a sure sign that they were expert computer users. Only die-hards and nerds, of varying degrees, frequented BBSs or the net.

Most ordinary people were reluctant to go online because they feared contracting computer viruses from downloads or messages. This fear was entirely misplaced, but users were accustomed to computers that were known to lock up for no apparent reason anyway, and the unseen risk of a virus was too much to add to the stress. The general phobia about viruses resulted in computer industry insiders considering the ARPANET, DARPANET, and BBSs as tools for professionals. Before the net can significantly affect the sales of computer software, the net must become universal. So long as the net is used by a minority of computer users, although it will be significant, it will not be the dominant force in development and retail.

Until recently, online services, like Compuserve or Prodigy (which eliminated the virus issue by scanning and verifying all files), were still curiosities unused by most computer owners. The fact that these services charged by the minute or hour discouraged most folks from ever fully experiencing their many offerings. Until flat-rate pricing for Internet access was available, only those with budgets for direct Internet access, or who worked or studied at large organizations with dedicated lines, could surf the net without panicking over the size of their bill.

No company took the lead in making the net what it is today. As with the initial wave of personal computer innovation, scientists and hobbyists led the way. No business or government agency decided to grow the net, and corporate America simply reacted to it. It all happened by itself, with home-based BBS sysops, the electronics nerds at public libraries, and experimental physicists leading the way. Hypertext markup language (HTML), now used to create web pages, was developed to aid nuclear physicists when sharing their latest experiences in atom smashing. The idea that millions of persons would share pictures of their family poodle using HTML documents on home pages was inconceivable to the persons who were on the net, even within the last few years.

Bill Gates's standard reply to arguments that Microsoft acts in monopolistic ways or manipulates the market is that end users and their opinion of the relative usefulness of computer systems determine what's successful, not corporate executives. Looking at the net as a test of Gates's hypothesis, this argument makes a great deal of sense, and Gates may be correct. Until the last ten years or so, the corporate view of the personal computer itself was that it was not commercially viable. And likewise it was too much of a leap for businesses to envision a world of networked computers. End users and hobbyists, and their microcomputers, brought the Internet to critical mass.

Microsoft, Netscape, and dozens of entrepreneurs have bet their corporate futures on Internet products, or even Internet domination. More commonly in the 1990s, the typical corporate strategy for innovation has become focused on the net. I liken the typical corporate strategy regarding innovation to "ready . . . fire . . . aim . . . retreat". A business-school example of this strategy is the affinity credit card, GM was one of the first companies to offer a credit card with a "rebate," which you could use to buy only their cars. GM secured many customers, but in October 1996, GM's undisclosed, but certainly large, liability incurred by the card effectively forced them to cut the benefits in half. Many other firms that created corporate affinity credit cards have entirely withdrawn from the market, including Apple Computers, which cloned the affinity card concept from GM.

The 1990s executive reads *Readers Digest*, too, and most no longer plunge right into ideas like affinity cards with reckless abandon only to lose money and, later, to see the company's stock jump two points when they announce withdrawal from the affinity card market or other fad. The late 1990s has bred a more cautious upper management. As a result, most businesses have waited longer to embrace the net and are more cautious about participating much further than with a home page. Having been burned by so many other new ideas, a level of timidity concerning any innovation, research, or development pervades industry.

However, the ice is thawing, and everyone today is interested in using the resources of the Internet. The Internet is a topic of discussion in the boardroom and in the lunchroom. If you try to see how important the Internet is by listening to public opinion, you may form an erroneous opinion of the size of the net. Try this experiment: go to any restaurant during lunch time, and keep as quiet as possible. Listen acutely to the conversations surrounding you. You will hear someone talk about the Internet within the first few minutes of active listening. Terms like web pages, net surfing, HTML, Active X, and Java have made it into the vernacular. This experiment will lead you to believe that the Internet is one of the most important public issues.

What does the computer industry itself think about the Internet? Winter Comdex 1996, the world's largest computer trade show, featured hundreds of Internet software magnate "wanna-bes." Hundreds of developers were hawking their Internet tools or systems. From this observation, you would correctly conclude that the software industry is extremely bullish on the Internet.

The next question to ask is how many people are on the net, and how many will be joining the net? To answer this question, you must determine the size of the Internet market first. The United States dwarfs all other markets for the number of Internet users and sites. Most countries have government monopolies in telephone service, and these phone companies impose heavy surcharges on Internet use. According to statements made by Reed Hundt, the Chairman of the U.S. Federal Communications Commission, the market penetration of Internet hosts is nearly three times greater, and dial-up Internet access is nearly three times cheaper, in the United States with its essentially deregulated Internet phone service than in countries with a monopoly phone company. Therefore, at present, the Internet market is the U.S. market.

Before reading the next few paragraphs, write down your estimate of the number of American households that are online. Your second pop-quiz question is true or false: "serious" Internet users are a *mass market* for software.

Industry observers make a distinction between serious Internet users and those who just exchange occasional e-mail or go to a web site now and then. The target for software sales is limited to the serious Internet user since the occasional or novice users have all the software that they may need, provided free by their Internet service provider (ISP).

One of the most astute observers of the online world is Jack Rickard of *Boardwatch Magazine*. A true telecommunications pioneer, Rickard is one of the most active participants in every aspect of telecommunications. He estimates that there are 25 million e-mail addresses in the United States, and that the core of serious Internet users is 11.6 million persons. How does 11.6 million persons compare with your estimate?

Jupiter Communications estimates that of the 98.9 million U.S. households, 38.7 million have PCs and 27.2 million of those homes have PCs equipped with modems. They estimate the number of households online, in any fashion, is 14.7 million. Jupiter predicts that in 1998, 47.8 million homes will have PCs and 27.3 million will be online, and that by the year 2000, 55.1 million homes will have PCs and 36 million will be online. It is impossible to estimate how many of the persons joining the net in the future will be serious Internet users. (If these estimates are correct, then the present market is dominated by one ISP, America Online. America Online's membership base is estimated at 8 million users by various sources in the financial and online community — over half of the nation's online households.)

If the number of households presently online is 14.7 million, and if 11.6 million persons are serious, that means that a very high number of the persons who try the net become serious. That indicates that, at least for the present, the prospect for new participants on the net becoming serious is excellent.

So, how'd you do on the quiz? These figures demonstrate that the community of serious Internet users is not yet a mass market. Market penetration of 10 percent would be required in order to reach a million sales in an 11-million-person market, and few applications reach this level of market penetration. The only application that presently has mass market potential is Internet browsers, which, it's safe to say, approximately 100 percent of Internet users must have. This market has one major difficulty: millions of copies of high-powered applications like Netscape's Navigator or Microsoft's Internet Explorer are being given away, both by ISPs and in software or hardware bundles. A market dominated by free software is not a great target for any market except the OEM market.

The next issue is how large the net will become later. We've already reviewed the estimates made by Jupiter Communications. *Communications Daily* estimates that over "the next few years" advertising on the Internet will increase by a factor of fifty, from $100 million to $5 billion. Reed Hundt's crystal ball says that the household penetration of the Internet will be as high as that of VCRs, telephones, and radios, which are 88, 95, and essentially 100 percent, respectively. Hundt recently stated at a technological conference:

How many radios do you have in your house today? You don't even know, right? That's the way it will be with Internet access devices in the reasonably near future. PC-stuff that will facilitate the access is all it takes. So the mini-PC's of the near future will be in your home's electrical equipment, your kid's book bag, attached to your belt, stuck in your brief case. You will have e-mail to your neighbors in the suburbs, or to the teacher in your kids' classes.

Hundt also notes that the enormous band width required to support this level of connectedness may come from cable, telephone, or LMDS satellite dishes. It is a matter of conjecture whether Hundt's view of a universal network or a more conservative view will prevail. Present information makes it difficult to determine whether the growth rate of the net will meet or exceed the present estimates.

For those who feel that the Internet can be "jump started" by a killer application that would create the market size needed to support mass market programs, here are some suggestions for the categories of programs that stand the best chance to be the killer applications for the net.

The application that has propelled the net is so far electronic mail. The worldwide hypertext web is also important in drawing users to the net, but e-mail has been the star.

There are several candidates for the next killer application for the net. If you can determine the killer application and develop it, you've created a multiple-million-copy seller. The one essential feature of the killer application for the net is that it must be a good fit between the computer and user. Computers can do many things that are irrelevant to users. As discussed in Chapter 2, many types of computer programs fail because computer programs aren't as good as other ways of achieving the same ends. No matter what the advantages are intellectually to the computer industry, unless substituting a computer for another appliance creates a huge advantage, the public will continue to use their present appliances.

ELECTRONIC SHOPPING

Every demographic and sociological factor favors more direct sales through twenty-four-hour catalogs. However, electronic shopping suffers from the same factors that limited computer end user participation in computer BBSs. Transferring money and credit card information over the network is still difficult. It is physically easier to fill out an order form and fax it than it is to fill out an online order form, and phoning to order a pizza is still easier than filling in a form on the net. This is a candidate, but not a strong one, for the next killer application.

BANKING AND STOCK TRADING

These activities are very similar to electronic shopping. The computer is an excellent way to do banking operations like paying bills or reconciling bank statements. However, until the fear of marauding Internet pirates is lessened, persons will prefer automatic tellers, direct deposit, and direct debits. Like electronic shopping, electronic banking may become a significant application area for OEM marketing. However, it is not the strongest contender.

ADULT INTERESTS

Gambling and sexual content are a good fit for the net. They are anonymous, available from all locations at all times, and reasonably good at sending images or betting information. The social stigma against both forms of recreation retards the growth of these "vices." However, personal desires and economic imperatives are so strong that these vices, or recreations, will become a dominant presence on the net. The opportunity for million-selling programs will not be providing the content, but providing the tools.

The antithesis of these adult interests, content filters or online "babysitters" that prevent children from accessing these sites, is a great idea as well. A market has already developed for content filters. However, there is still room for programs that are not as clumsy as some of the present entrants, which err on the side of caution and filter out too much.

ONLINE DATABASES

This area is a strong candidate for the killer application for businesses. The amount of financial and commercial intelligence available is staggering. Credit reports, marketing surveys, newsletters, and electronic editions of trade papers are receiving a great deal of attention from business Internet users. A killer application in this area might bring those businesspersons still on the fence into the arena.

TELECOMMUTING AND CONFERENCING

My intuition tells me that a new generation of tools to make secure meetings over the net just as good as being there in person is the killer application that will bring many persons to the net. Corporate downsizing has so effectively reduced costs that there are few areas left to make further cost cuts. Travel is one area that can quickly produce significant savings for an organization. Any combination of hardware and software that will make teleconferencing more effective will be eagerly accepted by the marketplace. Although IRC and Internet "telephones" already are available, a very low-cost, ultra high-quality meeting suite has huge potential in the future.

NEWSGATHERING

The first generation of intelligent agents are excellent sellers. "News tickers" that gather information and keep it updated continuously have the potential to be a killer Internet application. Bill Gates's *The Road Ahead* devotes much of its time to promoting a future in which intelligent agents are vital to the attractiveness of the Internet. My personal observation supports Gates's insight.

SCHOOL INTERNET SUITES

Hundt and many other leaders in both industry and government are committed to bringing Internet access into every postelementary school in the country. Hundt's present estimate of school access to the net is 9 percent. If the good intentions of the political figures are implemented, there will be a significant amount of money spent on making schools Internet ready. Schools will have unique demands to make on browsers, research, and e-mail. Given that there is talk of $15 billion to $20 billion being spent on building Internet infrastructure in schools, a significant dollar amount will be available for school-optimized net tools.

SOFTWARE MARKETING AND THE INTERNET

The most intriguing question about the Internet is how will it affect software marketing in the future? The first change will be lowering prices. If programs are delivered entirely on the net, the pricing of programs will drop to reflect the overall lower cost of production and distribution.

The price of consumer software has been steadily declining over the past five to six years. Many factors have contributed to this. One of the first was the suggestion by Jim Seymour that support costs had to be removed from the sale of computer programs. Seymour's articles in the late 1980s heralded the end of coupling support with the purchase price of mass market software and reduced the cost of software significantly.

WordPerfect, dBase, and others of the original generation of DOS supersellers sold for $495 or more when first released. However, all provided toll-free support. Most of that $495 was devoted to paying for support on the toll-free telephone lines. At one time, WordPerfect had to hire disc jockeys to entertain the persons who were on hold waiting for technical support. Many software developers spent many sleepless nights trying to figure out if their company could afford the ever-increasing phone bills and technical support overhead.

The decoupling of support from the sales price resulted in a drastic series of price cuts, as developers went from toll-free support to very limited regular phone support. Prices dropped from $495 to $199, then leveled off in the $79 to $99 range. Of course, many well-known applications still have list prices in the $400 range, but the list price of most applications is illusory. A "competitive upgrade" entitles almost anyone to buy at a much lower price.

Shareware distribution of programs and low-cost retail, usually at much lower prices than competitive commercial programs, whittled away at the concept of $495 or even $295 applications. In the late 1980s and 1990s, shareware and low-cost retail, with one or two exceptions, had programs as good as or better than their commercial counterparts at a lower price.

The Internet, once it is nearly universal, will produce a fundamental change in the pricing of computer programs. Since the first printing presses, publishers determined how to package books and how to price the information contained in them. Because of the tie-in to a physical product, paper and ink, the larger the book the higher the price. As an intangible commodity, the publisher decided how much information to give at a certain price. In addition, the fact that publishers take returns had to be factored into the price of the book. Even though there was a choice among books from different publishers on the same topic, the consumer was faced with a "take it or leave it" choice. Copyright laws reinforced the right of the author or publisher to set the terms and conditions of purchase.

As noted in Chapter 5, today the pricing and sale of computer programs closely parallels that of the book trade. However, if computer programs begin to be sold on the Internet in any significant numbers, the assumptions underlying the pricing of computer programs will no longer be accurate. It is so much cheaper to place programs on the net and let the customer get delivery of the file and manual in electronic form, that it seems inevitable computer programs will be distributed on the net electronically in a zero-sum game that directly subtracts from the number of programs sold in boxes.

The *user* will decide how much to pay for the program, rather than let the developer and retailer set the price. The Internet will allow the same program to be priced on a per use basis, buyout basis, or license basis. Industrial strength, regular, and "lite" versions of a program all can be stored on an Internet site, as easily as just one version of the program can be shelved now at a retail store. There will be no imperatives related to shelf space or returns for online delivery. As soon as a program is revised, the developer will release it, perhaps offering free, or pay-for download, updates for customers with older versions. You don't have to take back outdated binary bits in the same way that you do old boxed programs that have not sold.

However, it is very likely that the Internet sites will not be owned by the developer, but instead will be operated by existing retailers or new Internet-only retailers. Developers face the same problem in selling on the Internet as they do in conventional retailing. Unless you have the capital to extensively advertise, you must "give some of the action" to the retailer in exchange for drawing in customers. Software developers get the benefit of the capital investment in the stores and the stores' institutional advertising. In return, the developers give the store part of the profit. Developers will still need "referential advertising," by being placed on the shelf, or the Internet site, next to similar programs. A lone developer has little chance of attracting thousands of persons to their web site without expending huge sums of money. Therefore, distribution on the net will still typically be through retailers rather than directly from the manufacturer to the customer.

Every software entrepreneur must be aware that the Internet may change suddenly, and that no one within the industry really has any inkling about what will happen next to the net. "Protect yourselves at all times and come out fighting."

CHAPTER 9

▷ Shareware Marketing

Shareware is one of the most misunderstood concepts in the history of marketing of any product or service. The history of invention and innovation seems to follow a pattern described by Gil Hyatt, the person now credited, after a multidecade battle, as being the inventor of the microchip. Hyatt, like many inventors, personally has experienced being told that the invention is impossible; but then having the same persons claim that the invention was obvious *after* it succeeds. We will go through a detailed explanation of how shareware worked in the past and how it works at this time, and then show the powerful ways that shareware distribution can contribute to an overall marketing campaign.

Shareware is another of these "impossible but obvious" ideas that Hyatt referred to. In order to understand the concept of shareware, a brief history lesson about software in the early to mid-1980s is necessary. A few applications, like Lotus 1- 2- 3 and WordPerfect, were enormously popular, with a typical price of about $400 each at retail. This price point combined with several other factors that resulted to make shareware possible.

First, computers by the mid-1980s finally had disk drives so reliable that they were almost disk duplication machines. Although you might be bored while doing the work, making copies of programs was as simple as buying disks and taking the time to crank out copies. The price of disks plummeted, making copying even large programs a $5.00 investment in disks.

Second, computer software manufacturers bundled with their programs support on toll-free telephone lines. Because user interfaces were different from program to program and few persons understood software, toll-free support was popular and well patronized — so much so that WordPerfect hired disc jockeys to entertain users with estimates of the time to get to technical support and to chatter about the program. In an attempt to protect their investment in software, major software programs used copy protection to limit the number of times that master disks could be copied.

The need to maintain a retail price that was forty to sixty times the physical value of the materials used to create the program resulted in the laws of economics taking hold. People bought a few dollars worth of disks and made copies of software. Support was also not a significant motivation to encourage users to buy the goods at full price; this was particularly true when persons wanted to have a copy of the programs that they used at work for at-home use. A huge industry of how-to-use guides appeared in bookstores. To a great extent, the market for these books was created because the popular applications were very powerful, and the user guides provided by the manufacturers of the programs were not very good. Additionally, these third-party support guides were good enough to allow users to do without the user manuals provided with the programs.

Users were angered by the copy protection because they felt that they were *not* pirating software. Since the users' skills were a bit shaky, they tended to accidentally corrupt disks. In a more significant sense, users thought they were within their rights to have a copy of the same software on their home machines and on their office machines, as long as they used only one at a time. This interpretation of software licensing rights is also interesting in that it is very similar to Borland's "book model" license. It allowed the use of their program on one computer at a time, in the same way that a paper book could be taken between home and the office, but read by only one person at a time.

Entrepreneurs came up with two immediate reactions to the public's need for ease of duplication on the one hand and copy protection on the other. The first was "if a computer did it, another computer can undo it." A thriving industry in "uncopy protect" software appeared. Manufacturers who used copy protection routines fought the uncopy protect programs in court because they couldn't seem to fight it by counterprogramming against the "unlock" schemes. The legal battle culminated in the Quaid Software decision by the U.S. Court of Appeals for the Fifth Circuit, upholding the legality of uncopy protect software.

Another group of programmers came up with another idea: shareware. Andrew Flugelman and Jim Button are credited with being the creators of shareware. A rigorous definition of shareware is necessary so that we can explain how to consider using shareware as part of an integrated marketing plan. Shareware is software just like other commercial computer software. Shareware is copyrighted and thus, under section 106 of the Copyright code, is protected like any other copyright work. However, the developer agrees to waive some of the rights. Flugelman and Button distributed software and encouraged people to give away copies of their programs. These programs weren't without cost. Users were asked to pay a "registration fee" in exchange for getting ownership of the program. Some shareware authors took the approach of asking for "donations." Because software sold in stores was protected from being opened by shrink-wrapping them shut, a new term was coined to describe traditional computer software. "Shrink-wrap" software was used to refer to computer software that was sold in stores.

The concept was very exciting to users, and Button and Flugelman created excellent programs that were equal to their commercial competitors. Flugelman coined the term *freeware* to describe software that could be copied and obtained a trademark for freeware. After Flugelman's death, because of legal concerns, Button's term, *shareware*, was used to describe this software that was legal to be "shared." Shareware was also priced lower than store-bought shrink-wrap programs because there was no middleman. Users bought direct. Most shareware registration fees in the early days were significantly lower than shrink-wrap software. In most cases, shareware registration fees were $29, $39, or $59 when the dominant programs charged $299 to $495. Shareware had a great deal going for it — low-cost, good-quality programs that were "friendlier" than shrink-wrap programs. Various information pieces about shareware stated "shareware has the ultimate money-back guarantee — don't pay unless you know that the program meets your needs." In fact, Button's early manuals for PC-File asked people if they didn't like the program to give the evaluation disk to someone who might use it rather than erase the disk. Selling software on trust sounded crazy, but as many shareware authors can attest to, when they open the mailbox, they find checks and orders.

Indeed, in most cases, the author did the technical support. Users who heard about shareware found that they could get almost any program they wanted in shareware. Shareware went from a "crazy" idea to a successful niche business for those who worked as hard at shareware as other companies worked on shrink-wrap software. Most authors didn't invest the time needed to really make it, or their programs were weak. However, strong programs could get verified sales of shareware disks numbering in the millions worldwide. During 1991 and 1992, my Home and Business Legal Guide had verified distribution, through those vendors who were willing to share data, of well over 500,000 yearly copies, while occupying *PC Source* magazine's second to fourth position on the "Top 10" sales lists.

An extensive distribution network for these programs appeared. BBSs like EXEC-PC, the largest microcomputer-based BBS in the world, collected thousands of files. User groups built extensive libraries of evaluation versions of software. In the days when many small local BBSs competed for callers, great excitement was generated whenever new versions of favorite programs, like PK ARC and PK ZIP, were released. Competition occurred between different shareware distributors to have the latest versions of programs first.

Authors flocked to shareware. Here was a channel where hard work and a little money, rather than hard work and huge amounts of money, could lead to sales. One of the more interesting spinoff industries, shareware disk vendors, opened and sold collections of disks. Public Brand Software, Shareware to Go, and other vendors distributed hundreds of thousands of catalogs of rated and reviewed shareware, and sold millions of disks. An author who could get registration rates of one in a thousand might sell several thousand copies of his or her program. To make a success in shareware, the concept was to saturate the market with evaluation disks and then develop a mailing list, and follow with improved versions of the software to earn additional revenue.

Once a customer list is built, a shareware author can count on substantial reorders for improved versions of their programs. A base of several thousand users is like an annuity — the investment on obtaining the users produces yearly income through selling upgrades or additional services, just like an annuity. These types of programs are called either "evergreen programs" or "annuitized programs." Every expert on marketing will agree that it is much less expensive to retain customers and make further sales to them than it is to get new customers.

Many authors used their shareware as low-cost traveling salespeople. Although some authors didn't make a living from shareware alone, custom programming work and consulting did allow them to operate profitable businesses. But there was another good thing that happened to shareware authors. Publishers of commercial software started to scout shareware for programs to publish commercially and for programmers or development teams to hire. Many authors find that shareware is an apprenticeship to traditional distribution, or as effective as using agents. Authors of books learn that having an agent is necessary to get a book reviewed by a publisher. There are almost as many books on how to get an agent as there are on how to write your best-seller. Stories about "slush piles" and "over the transom" books being published — once every twenty years — aren't applicable to shareware authors.

The difficulty with shareware becoming a larger force in the market is that despite the efforts of disk vendors, the Association of Shareware Professionals (ASP), and online services, even those within the computer industry don't grasp the basic idea. Shareware is a different way of looking at marketing, and just as there are good and bad programs sold in shrink-wrap, there are good and bad shareware programs. Shareware isn't a type of software.

Two other important events occurred. At the same time that many software companies were charging hundreds of dollars for programs, a small group of entrepreneurs realized that the intrinsic cost of the software, a few disks, a manual, and a carton was so small compared to the sales prices, that software would come down in price over time. The "low-cost retail" market appeared at the same time as shareware. Pioneers in low-cost retail, like shareware authors, starting selling software for much less than others, creating an entire industry. Budget software publishers frequently teamed up with shareware authors. The budget market is now a mature one, with several of the top twenty publishers in unit sales being budget companies.

Budget software and low-cost retail have suffered from "perceived value" problems. Phrases like "you get what you pay for" encourage persons to assume that price reflects the quality of goods. Insiders know better. Although there may be a case for this at the beginning of the budget industry, by the end of the 1980s the quality of budget titles became equal to other channels. The only difference between expensive and inexpensive software is the market niche picked by the authors. In fact, many companies have taken the "General Motors" approach of a "program for every purse" and produce low-cost, middle-cost, and high-cost versions of their program, for both commercial and shareware.

Authors developed a variety of registration incentives to try to improve the results of the "trust the user to register to pay" syndrome. Although the shareware market has matured, these same strategies are still in use.

SUPPORT

Most shareware authors provide special levels of support for registered users. Not offering support to unregistered users is not a good idea. Callers who want support are potential customers. Shareware authors obtain significant numbers of registrations because the caller naturally feels a level of gratitude for receiving assistance. Shareware authors stress that in most cases, because they are small shops, you get customer support from an expert — the person or persons who wrote the program. Compare this with large software companies who offer "pay per call" service only.

LIMITED MANUALS

Jim Button's PC-File program originally blocked out certain portions of the manual. Enough was left to allow the user to test the program. This no longer is used, particularly because the idea of shareware is that the user should enjoy using the program. If they are one of the few users who actually read the manual, they will be irritated if answers to their questions are blocked out. However, even with fast Internet lines, large download times can discourage persons from obtaining the software to evaluate. Therefore, many shareware programs substitute online help for manuals.

CRIPPLING

Crippling is withholding features in order to encourage users to register. This is the most controversial registration incentive. The "gospel" from the shareware experts until recently was that crippling was counterproductive. The

Association of Shareware Professionals originally enforced a strict anticrippling rule, requiring the registered and unregistered programs to be essentially the same. This policy caused defections from the ASP, and in a recent change in policy, the ASP now permits some crippling.

NAG SCREENS

These are opening or closing, or both, screens that encourage the user to register. Some nag screens require users to wait for several seconds to enter or exit the program. Another variation of a nag screen is a "key press" screen. These require that the user enter different keystroke combinations to continue using the program. Nag screens can occur while the programming is running or at signon or exit. Nag screens are considered by industry insiders to be ways to get your software erased rather than registered.

PRINTED MANUAL

Surveys show that printed manuals are among the items that users want the most.

UPGRADES

Many programs offered reduced price or free upgrades to later versions.

KARMA

Many programs have screens imploring people to be honest and register if they use the program. Some also include humor like "the author has been known to play the tuba late at night in front of the homes of users who don't register."

DAY/USE SCREENS

These screens indicate the days or number of times the program has been used. The hope is that the users will see that they are making significant use of the program and will have their honor intensified. Shareware insider, and now head of the shareware collections for the Microsoft Network, Paul Mayer, reports that he receives many registrations when his shareware payroll system gets to "29 days out of 30 days."

PUBLIC EXPOSURE

Shareware programs that develop output that a customer uses, can be coded to announce that the program is not registered. Many computer BBSs are marketed through shareware and show that the system is "unregistered." This is a very effective way to encourage users to register after a reasonable period of testing and evaluation.

NETWORKS/PEER GROUPS

When BBS systems were more popular than the Internet, some shareware publishers would only carry networked user messages for registered users. Others developed special user meetings or conventions just for registered users. For complex software, a closed convention or a message system on the Internet, or on dial-up BBS systems, is still a significant inducement to registration.

SOURCE CODE

Some of the most successful shareware programs offer users source code if they register. This is effective particularly if the shareware is used by programmers or in mission-critical applications. Providing source code gives a level of comfort to the users that if all else fails they can tweak the source code.

LOCK OUTS

After a specified number of uses or days of use, the program locks the user out. This is not a significant incentive if a person is willing to reinstall the program, with the exception of database or accounting programs. However, many users will take the program's statement that the program will no longer work literally.

SPECIAL OFFERS

ASP authors offered free Compuserve sign-up kits. Other shareware developers offered special tie-ins to encourage registration. These tie-ins have varied from Internet service to admission to annual conventions.

EPISODES

The most effective registration incentive for game shareware is to release the initial levels of play, but only give further levels of play after payment. Duke Nukem and Quake from id software have become major commercial and shareware successes by offering the first round of play, but holding back others until payment. id's 1996 release of Quake started off, in addition to traditional shareware marketing, with 500,000 retail, $6 to $7 CD-ROMs containing part one of four parts of the Quake games. The only sell through figures released indicate that about half of the shareware demonstration disks were sold. id also promised to make a payment to retailers if their customers registered. Industry sources have reported 25,000 registrations at $50 each, approximately 10 percent of the retail purchasers, in addition to full-price retail sales. This represents a sizable, although not mass market, performance. This concept can work with almost every kind of program. Although it's a form of crippling, the user does have a reasonable opportunity to use the program before committing dollars to obtain the rest of the program, which is well within the shareware spirit.

The Association of Shareware Professionals was created to attempt to standardize the programming practices within the shareware industry. The ASP seeks to explain the concept of shareware to the public and to further the public's confidence level in shareware authors and programs. The ASP still requires that authors provide specific levels of support and provides an ombudsman to settle disputes between authors and their users. ASP software's certification marks many serious shareware authors. In recent years, a relaxation of the rules on crippling reduced the rate of authors defecting.

To cripple or not to cripple? Shareware that I have personally been involved with did *not* cripple at all. The programs were traditionally distributed in two versions, a short "sampler" as well as the full program. The purpose of the sampler was to allow persons with slow modems to be able to obtain the file within a reasonable length of time. Even with 28,800 baud and faster modems, users can be reluctant to commit to downloading large files. However, a number of interesting comments have led me to reconsider releasing uncrippled software.

Although not scientific, we received registrations regularly from users who couldn't print or perform other normal program functions, who registered only because they assumed that their problems resulted from intentional crippling. Our shareware insider, Paul Mayer, has recently recommended both lock outs and some level of crippling to encourage registrations.

ASP has created an excellent distribution network for their programs. CD-ROMs and electronic distribution are made available to shareware vendors, BBSs, and online electronic distribution services. ASP authors grant more or less blanket permission to ASP disk distributors to distribute their files. Shareware authors are a rather independent lot, and many require shareware distributors to go through hoops to get permission to distribute files. This is a very bad idea since the key to having a reasonable chance to become a success in shareware is massive distribution. Some shareware libraries have hundreds of thousands of files and, as a result, feel no compulsion to work with any particular author.

A number of the most successful programmers within the shareware industry did not accept ASP guidelines. In particular, there are shareware developers who have insisted on crippling and extensive use of registration incentives not within ASP guidelines. Many of these are among the most successful in the business.

Shareware is viable either as an end to itself or as another way to obtain revenue and publicity. Every publisher, from small ones to the largest, scouts shareware formally or informally. Publishers look through shareware both for programs to publish and for talented programmers. Shareware authors with good distribution had, and still have, an interested audience with money to spend looking at their software. The reason is that the development cycle in software is measured in weeks, not months.

Paper books generally take nine months from conception to delivery. Even "instant" books like those produced following the O. J. Simpson trials, require a month to make it to the market. A determined software publisher can (and I have) gone from concept to product in a week. But the only way to do that is to have completed software. Publishers at software houses fret and become interested in coming out with their own version of anything that appears to sell or even have the potential to sell. The odds are that in almost every category of software there are already extant shareware programs, and since momentum is a key buzzword in software as in football, in order to seize the day, software publishers look to the existing software if they need a title.

From a business standpoint, commissioning a program is a $10,000 to $40,000 minimum commitment — and usually much more than that. If the program is ready, the publisher gains speed in the attack or counterattack. Since the cost of development has been borne by the shareware author, both parties benefit, the developer by additional revenue and the software publisher by obtaining an immediate title.

The strategy of "worm" programming, "Write Once, Resell Many Times" was perfected by many programmers. This can include using the same basic engine to power different programs or renaming and refeaturing a basic program in different editions for different markets.

Shareware has a bad name among many software authors. A significant number of software authors don't want to "give away" anything. This ignores the fact that users copy programs, and avoids the publicity and "silent sales force" advantages that shareware distribution offers. Many authors have tried shareware but received few registrations. These same authors assume that the shareware system doesn't work. In almost every case, the program would have failed whether a commercial or a shareware product. The failure rate of commercial shrink-wrap software for almost all programs is identical to the failure rate of shareware for almost all programs. The shareware "miss" rate is significantly affected by the fact that many shareware programs reflect a poor choice of subject matter because the shareware author was a good programmer but not a good marketing manager.

Commercial shrink-wrap software must be sold several times before it hits the shelves. If a program is published for an author by a publisher, the publisher must be convinced that the program has a market niche. The same process is repeated since the program is presented to buyers at retail locations, wholesalers, and manufacturers' representatives. Shareware programmers sometimes write code for months without discussing the program's market potential with anyone.

Another reason that many shareware authors don't do well is that they do not approach shareware distribution as a serious business. Too many authors have created a program, placed it on a few online services, and then waited for registrations to roll in. Shareware distribution works only if the author achieves the greatest possible distribution of a good concept. The most successful shareware authors take extensive steps to ensure that their programs are offered everywhere that they can be. This includes keeping in close touch with other shareware authors to obtain new sources for distribution.

One of the best bets for shareware programs is "filling in the gaps" of bestselling commercial software. Regardless of the amount of programming invested in commercial software, there are always awkward functions or missing features. A number of shareware authors do an excellent business by providing functions that the programmers of well-known programs forgot.

To reach mass market sales figures, every possible mode of distribution should be used. If you have any question whether shareware is a good idea, consider that a new wrinkle on shareware has sprung up around Internet browsers and tools. Netscape and Microsoft's Internet Explorer have been available for downloading with minimum effort. If it looks like shareware and sounds like shareware, it must be shareware. It's another crazy idea. Some users may buy the deluxe versions of the browser. These companies are also counting on income from "side effect sales" of the tools to make software that uses the browsers. Like shareware pioneers, it seems like "giving something away" is bad business. It is not. Shareware distribution is an investment in exposure of a program, and the programmers who wrote it, to end users and to the industry.

A computer program is a resource that must be managed in the same way that other intellectual property is treated. Consider the music industry. Music publishers receive only small payments from broadcasters for the right to play their artists' songs on the air. Music publishers count on the exposure they receive from being broadcast to get the public to buy the CDs and tapes that generate the bulk of their revenue.

A program is worth nothing if it is not in distribution of some kind. Like bread, a computer program is perishable and gets stale. Shareware is a market channel separate from the shrink-wrap industry although it is related. Renamed and refeatured "channel conflict" is not a significant issue for shareware programs.

The Internet is now established as the dominant mode of distribution for shareware although user groups, BBSs, and disk vendors are still important ways to obtain distribution. A good web site, and posting programs to hot sites, can get programs into the hands of potential customers. All the positives definitely outweigh any perceived negatives, and like General Motors, reaching every possible market for your programs makes any work that you do on shareware an excellent investment.

Experts on entrepreneurship have always recommended "incremental" product introduction, releasing discrete parts of the firm's product as each section is ready. The benefits are that the entrepreneur is able to gain some revenue and operational experience rather than being a "concept only" entity. Shareware allows program developers a chance to "test drive" their program while building recognition and revenue.

PART III

▷ **Operating
Issues**

CHAPTER 10

▷ Retaining Market Share

Once your program is released, the battle is not over; in fact, the war has just begun. Just surviving at retail long enough to get the first reorder requires constant vigilance. Growing a program to a best-seller is yet more difficult. Unfortunately, more than half the titles released in retail are returned with minimal sales — a fate worse than never having been released at all. The cost to launch a title in retail nearly matches development costs. After slotting fees, marketing development funds, and direct material cost of production, the net result of a failed program on the balance sheet is much worse than if nothing was done after completing the program. Of the surviving titles, most won't make it to six-digit sales levels, much less a million units.

Success in software sales is measured by net sales performance. The cost of marking down slow-moving goods, or accepting returns, has killed many successful companies. In my experience, after a title does well, within three months two publishers will have a shareware or previous program in the category republished. Within nine months, a successful title will draw ten to twenty copy cats trying to get "a piece of the pie." To reach success, you will have to deal with numerous competitors. Unfortunately, good publishers can use any mistakes that you made, or your gambles that didn't pay off, as their field research for a better shot at the same market — thus, the winnowing process between programs completed and programs that make it to retail.

Releasing the program to retailers is like the old adage about leading a horse to water. Selling what you place in the various marketing channels is making the horse drink. You must fend off challengers and devote as much effort to managing a program after release as you did during design.

To retain shelf space at retail, programs must meet targets for sell through. There are two types of targets for sell through. The first type is explicitly set in contracts and purchase orders; almost every retailer has a "vendor manual" that usually includes sell through standards. The second is that a retailer cannot be compelled to reorder any specific title, or for that matter, any title at all from a publisher. If any title doesn't sell through, a retailer may condition reorder of other titles on taking back unsold product, or allowing markdown refunds so that the products can be sold for below the wholesale price to just dispose of them. Anticipate that whatever the formal terms of sale may state, it is an unwritten term that you will have to make allowances for poor-selling programs.

Minimum turn rates are similar among retailers in the same type of retail operation. Here are some typical minimum turn rates. (A store month is one calendar month in one store; generally, turn rates are calculated as an average across an entire chain since some locations have more traffic than others.)

Computer specialty stores: 3 per SKU per store month

Mall-based retailers: 1.5 per SKU per store month

Mass merchandisers: 2 per SKU per store month

Low-price mass merchandisers: 4 per SKU per store month

Warehouse clubs: 6 per SKU per store month

Mail order: 20 per catalog entry per store month

Before selling to a retailer, ensure that you have a specific commitment for acceptable turn levels and reorders. Planning for managing returns and obtaining reorders is the difference between success and failure. Many software developers are willing to take any orders that they get. However, success is measured by sell through, not placement. Before committing resources to any retailer, consider whether or not the order will sell through. By explicitly discussing reorders and turn levels before committing to a sales relationship, you can avoid entering into poor deals.

By discussing turn rates and reorders before making the sale, you can reach an informed decision on the target sell through rates that you will require to make an acceptable return on the investment in slotting fees and MDF requested by the retailer. The most critical sales management error in the software publishing field is taking any order that comes by and hoping that the programs can be sold.

In addition to considering the overriding topic of sell through, you must consider what the cost of the market share will be. Include in your calculations the requested slotting fees and other commitments asked for by each retailer. Sell through obtained by agreeing to a slotting fee that is too high can result in a million sales without much profit to show for the effort. This is proved by the fact that several publicly traded software companies sell about $30 million in product but still operate at a loss. Yes, it is possible to have an unprofitable best-seller.

Even though telephones, faxes, and e-mail are the ways that developers normally communicate with retailers and wholesalers, physical inspection of retail outlets is vital. Do your store checks before accepting orders from that retailer. These visits, if carefully planned, produce vital intelligence to help you predict sell through.

Do a store check to observe how many cashiers are working. Some outlets, the ones where you need to fight the hardest to obtain the most space, are mobbed and are the best targets for ultra high-volume sales. My own inspections have uncovered some 70,000-square-foot gigantic stores that have only one or two cashiers working (except during Christmas), whereas other stores of the same size have a minimum of ten cashiers working at a time, and thirty or forty at peak times over weekends. The first is a poor bet for sell through; the second a store that will justify a significant investment.

While visiting your potential sales partners, check the appearance of the product displays.

- Are the sales shelves neat and detailed? A neat presentation of programs is vital to sales. In some outlets, the products are not marked with prices, and the only way to tell the price of the program is to match it to the shelf tag. If programs are not stocked in the right position, the customers won't know the price. Unless they are willing to hunt down a salesperson to scan the product's price, they probably will not buy your program.

- Is the store stocking the latest versions of the programs? Unless the section is an "oldenware" one, a store that has too many older versions either isn't up to date or isn't selling.

- How many markdowns are there? In the software field, almost any markdown on the shelf indicates that the program's developer has given a partial refund to the retailer for "price protection." A great deal of marked down merchandise doesn't bode well for the new entrants.

- Are there special promotions and displays? If a retailer has special stand-alone displays dedicated to single product lines, you can probably make similar arrangements — for a price.

An excellent guide to picking retailers that make the most concentrated effort is the *Computer Retail Weekly* yearly listing of the top one hundred retail outlets for hardware and software sales. You should estimate the number of facings that each outlet has in an average store, then divide this by their reported software sales volume and number of stores to estimate the average sales per SKU. This gives you a rough guide to which retailers can sell the greatest number of copies of your software.

Like other industries, software has an 80/20 rule: 20 percent of the customers produce 80 percent of the business. This has proved to be true over time for most retailers. Concentrate your efforts on the outlets that show the best sales performance.

Part of the reengineering movement suggests that companies make long-term partnershiplike arrangements with suppliers for maximum flexibility in delivery and quality. Karl Sabbagh's book on the building of the Boeing 777, *Twenty-First-Century Jet*, is valuable reading on how to create and manage true team relationships with vendors. Close working relationships foster a willingness to engage in stock balancing and to work together to create mutual concessions in the case of (well-intentioned) failures. Personal relationships are valuable in the software business. Whatever the corporate imperatives are for goals and performance between the parties, if you're in a tight spot, it's useful to both publisher and retailer to have favors to call in. Thus for selfish reasons, be sure to build a long-term relationship with your retailers. You will all need to work together when it's time to engage in stock balancing.

The publishing business is one where illogical things happen. No matter how hard persons try and no matter what their level of experience, great plans don't always work. Even if every fiber in your being tells you that this program is *the one*, remember that just the process of getting approval to be published makes your program part of a small, elite group. Even programs in this exclusive group have a more than 50 percent chance of being returned without great levels of sales. You must have a plan B in case the title fails. We will discuss fine-tuning a title that is close to meeting sell through goals in this chapter, but the release of any title must be accompanied by a realistic strategy for retreat if it fails.

Returns are terrible. Outright returns are ruinous. Stock balancing, in which slow-selling product is swapped for other goods, is still bad for the bottom line, but not as bad as outright returns. Have another product ready so that, if results aren't satisfactory, the slotting fee invested in shelf space isn't wasted.

A typical fully stocked computer retailer will carry from five hundred to a thousand titles. Most mass merchants carry forty to a hundred titles, whereas warehouse clubs carry fewer than forty but change their mix constantly. In any case, normally, less than half of the titles are meeting the minimum turn rate. That means hundreds of programs have made it to retail but will not be a success. This problem causes significant expense for all concerned. Recent articles in the computer sales trade papers have confirmed that, like hardware, software has an average return rate of about 20 percent. This high a rate of return on product that is typically marked up by only 20 percent is disastrous. Consider that the 20 percent average is not the modal value; it is reached by software selling no copies being averaged with software that sells out and a general return rate of 40 to 50 percent. The overall rate is so low because the winners sell every copy and dwarf the other sales.

It's difficult to think about having another program ready in case your title fails. After all, if a development team isn't passionate about the potential for a title it wouldn't invest the energy to release the title. But the law of averages favors the survival of those who have a plan B.

Many factors together determine sell through of any individual title at retail. (I will consider the effect that competitors have on programs separately.)

INFORMATION ON SELL THROUGH

Despite UPC readers at the cash register and perpetual inventories, some retailers do not provide sell through information to publishers. This is especially a problem if the retailer is buying the program from a distributor. Be sure that retailers and wholesalers provide you with sell through figures as often as they can. Weekly sell through figures are ideal. These allow you to plan immediately in the event that a program is below the target sell through rates. If the news is good, you can keep your program in stock by getting reorders.

PRODUCT MIX AT A SPECIFIC RETAILER

Some programs do outstanding sell through at one retailer and very poor at another. This is caused by one of two factors: failure to stock or the product mix at that retailer. No two retailers have the same titles. In one location, you may be the only spreadsheet on the shelf, at another, your spreadsheet program may be one of a dozen. Sometimes a retail chain decides that a particular category of program is going to be hot and then buys everything in that category. Sales will obviously be higher in outlets where you have fewer competitive titles.

Pass on selling to retailers clogged with competitive titles. There are so many channels and outlets for your programs that you can reach a million sales without being in every retail outlet. A few bad accounts can eat up the profit from new ones. As noted, field research at retailers is vital to determining whether or not to launch a title. It is good business strategy to hold off on placing your program at an outlet that has a huge supply of competing titles until you have established that you have a winner; in the meantime, you can concentrate on less competitive outlets. After all, buyers read sales figures in *PC-Research* too. By doing well in some venues, you will open the doors to others. If your program does extremely well at your "cherry-picked" outlets, you will be in a stronger bargaining position to get your title into other outlets — without your competition! This doesn't mean that you should avoid placing your program in direct competition with similar titles. It does mean that you should give your program the best chance of making it by waiting for publicity and sell through at outlets that aren't flooded with your title's competition.

FAILURE TO STOCK AT RETAIL

Some retailers have goods shipped directly to centralized warehouses; others have inventory drop-shipped to individual stores. In each case, several additional steps are required to make the program actually available for sale to customers. The goods must be placed on the shelves, the shelves must be marked with your product's name, and perhaps price stickers must be added to the packages. Any other display items negotiated between the parties, such as shelf talkers, must also be implemented. Unfortunately, from time to time, goods are not placed on shelves, or they languish in a warehouse. If sell through is poor, verify by physical inspections that your programs are in fact on the shelf in the right area. A variation on this problem is that your program sells out and is not reordered. Obviously, you can't meet a minimum turn rate if a retailer doesn't buy enough copies of your program to sell. This highlights the importance of having accurate, timely sell through information. If a title is going well, getting reorders is vital. Remember too that retailers generally operate on just-in-time principles, so reorders are likely to be in small enough quantity that there will not be returns.

PUBLICITY AND AWARENESS

If favorable reviews of your products appear in high-circulation magazines, sales increase directly because of public awareness of the product. For example, antiviral software experiences sales jumps when viruses that activate on specific dates are publicized in the media. These events require extremely good inventory management to ensure that your program is in sufficient supply at just the right time.

EXTERNAL FORCES, SUCH AS OPERATING SYSTEM CHANGES

The largest vendors in the computer industry make announcements of anticipated releases of new technology and operating systems long before the anticipated release date. All industry insiders believe that these "vaporware"
announcements encourage purchasers to procrastinate. During the 1996
Christmas season, every retail marketing executive quoted in the trade press said
that hardware sales were soft because of the impending January 8, 1997, release
date of Intel's MMX brand processor. Consumers had an excellent reason to wait
until tomorrow to buy a computer. If there is any constant in a technology-dri-
ven business like software, it is that computers will become less expensive and
more powerful over time. Retail buyers will always regret their purchase because,
within a few months, they will see something better for the same price. The resis-
tance to commitment peaks during technology changeovers. This is a very close
call to make, but generally getting a program to market sooner is the best bet. An
easy way to counteract the problem of "planned obsolescence" in software is to
offer a free upgrade to the next version. A related problem is having software for
an operating system or chip that is not yet on the market. Nevertheless, you must
consider the big picture and take steps to accommodate the next change in technology in timing releases. You have only one chance to keep shelf space. If you
release a program and it fails, it is virtually impossible to get on the shelf. Choose
carefully when to start your sales campaign at any specific retailer.

SEASONAL FACTORS

Whether or not consumers see computer software as a seasonal item, retailers
order more during August and December, and less during January and July.
This indicates that computer software is coming closer and closer to being an
ordinary commodity rather than a specialty item. Many computer companies
do not release programs during the slowest times of the year on the theory that
the program may be delisted (discontinued) because sales are slow generally.
Other companies release programs any time of the year, or even favor releasing
programs when the number of new titles is at its lowest. I feel that a good title

will sell all times of the year, though in fewer quantities during slower times, and that this factor is overrated by some software companies.

If you have determined that sell through is not up to the standards that you expect, take immediate action. You can do several things to improve sell through. The solution to this difficulty is to determine the basic problem. First, you must verify that product is being properly displayed and kept in stock. Is the retailer capable of handling stocking and reorders of the software? Aberrations may occur in even the best organizations; however, retailers who are failing will have recurring problems with keeping goods in stock. Credit managers within the software field can predict slow-pay accounts or chargeoffs by seeing how well the retailer manages stock. If you are dealing with a retailer that has logistical problems, you must decide whether to continue sales or, perhaps, take matters in your own hands by using detailing companies.

Detailing companies perform physical checks of store locations, prepare inventories, and ideally, immediately restock all goods to your desired stocking level. By a combination of reports and restocking, detailers can sometimes correct deficiencies occurring at the point of sale. Like obtaining placement by paying slotting fees, detailing is an expense that must be justified by return on investment. Detailing sounds like a great idea, particularly if a retailer is not keeping everything up to date. However, store checks can cost $40 or $50 each and result in a crushing expense. Consider that some chains have more than two thousand locations each. Do you have an extra $100,000 per month ($1.2 million per year) just for detailing? Adding to the complexity and expense of detailing is how often the display should be checked. If detailing is done once a month, there is still a good possibility that the product will be sold out or misshelved within a few days.

Another way to increase market share is to market to the sales forces in the retail locations. As the computer software market matures, the battle for market share will become more fierce. To gain market share, direct work at point of sale will become the last battleground. This can range from purchasing ads in trade magazines to providing live or videotaped classes on the features of your program to sales personnel. Those within the industry do not realize the importance of salespeople. Many customers will buy based solely on store sales personnel's recommendations.

An interesting idea used by some publishers is a "secret shopper" contest in which the publisher sends out "shoppers" to test the product knowledge of sales personnel, rewarding those who correctly describe program features with prizes. In late 1996, several manufacturers of hardware assigned their own salespeople to work at retail stores to ensure that their products are given the best chance to sell through. The dollar amount of a hardware transaction is normally higher than software, so it is more difficult to justify that expense for software. However, a roving team of demonstrators will easily pay for itself in mass market sales. Warehouse clubs and other "high-volume" outlets are ideal targets for demonstrations.

If sales are not adequate, placing the title in a special promotion may increase sales volume. Promotions are special sales events that are run for a limited time and feature special placement. Promotions may be placed in "power aisles" or in special fixtures. Contests, special pricing, or rebates are also used with promotions. But remember that a poor contest adds nothing to sales, and unfortunately, there are many poorly designed promotions.

Another strategy for increasing sell through is combining slower-selling titles with faster-selling ones in multiple packs. The drawback of this is recalling product. Multiple program packs may not fit in displays made for single products. This practice costs a great deal of money and requires a recall of the software on the shelf. Be sure to verify that your publication contract permits royalty splitting on combined packages. Boilerplate agreements do not generally cover division of royalties in the event of joint publication.

Some publishers cut the price of programs if they don't achieve acceptable sell through. This is a poor idea. If a program fails to sell at the original price point, it is because the program's topic or features are wrong. A bad $49 program will fail at $19. The only success stories in cutting prices are when the program is renamed and repackaged. The reason that the second try works is the repackaging rather than the price cut.

Every successful program encourages copy cats. Some are blatant attempts to retread the same concept. Others may be improvements on your concept. But any type of competitor is a serious challenge to consider. The best policy for keeping your program's market share is to work diligently at replacing your own title. This means that the day after shipping your program, you have to sit down and design a program that is much better. If your best competition is your own organization, you are well on the way to creating a million-seller.

We must first define what products compete with one another. Being the same type of program (for example, word processors) places two products in competition. But you must also consider whether the program on a similar topic results in a channel conflict. Two shoot 'em up games with a street price of $29 are competitors. However, two shoot 'em up games, one priced at $9.99 and the other priced at $49.99, do not represent the same level of channel conflict. The purchasers of $50 games and $10 games are two different groups of consumers. The publishers of $50 games and $10 games should be aware of one another, but they are not in direct competition.

Every program is going to be replaced in the marketplace by another, given enough time. The key to making a success of your business is to make yourself your own strongest competition. Doing so will result in both your designing improvements to your existing program and ultimately starting a new program with a fresh design.

This is perhaps the hardest decision a publisher faces, and deciding when to replace a program with an improved edition is made even more difficult because so many factors affect the decision. Ideally, a publisher could, when an improved edition of the program is available, immediately put that new edition in circulation. This "raises the bar" and gives a company that is aggressive in giving value to customers an advantage in the marketplace. The problem is there are severe side effects created by changing versions of a program.

Every retail software sales contract provides that the developer must recall any unsold older product when a new edition makes existing stock obsolete. As noted in other chapters, there is a new tendency not to return product, but to "remainder it in place," which means that the publisher must give a credit to the retailers to cover markdowns. Therefore, releasing a new version of a program results in a financial commitment to recall the stock of the older program or to make refunds to retailers. Compounding the financial loss is that the programs sold at remaindered prices usually entitle their purchasers to the new version at a discount.

If smaller changes are made in a program not constituting a "new version," the developer can normally use stickers. One strategy is to offer a "limited time" bonus of the new feature, and then, when stock dwindles, replace it with the newer title, with the limited-time features relabeled as standard features. The larger question is whether small changes have any significant effect on sales.

Andy Grove, the chief executive officer of Intel, in his recent apology, *Only The Paranoid Survive*, states that corporations must be aware of strategic inflection points. These are critical points when change is so powerful that you must react. Strive to be the moving party in change, not a bystander. Obviously, the best outcome is when the changes are within your control. Grove offers an excellent insight that he refers to as "10X," or ten-times, changes. These occur when a new technology appears that makes changes on the order of ten times the previous technology. As a result, when a change on the power of ten occurs, the impossible becomes trivial. If you have a 10X change, whatever losses may come from recalling your stock of older programs, release the new version and create a new standard.

In the software industry, these changes occur in a manner very similar to what Groves must contend with as a chip maker. I have always tried to raise the level between releases to create a preemptive strike, or "complete one-upmanship." This means that changes must be gigantic. Your goal is to create a new version of already good software that is so overwhelmingly superior that competitors lose interest in the area. When overwhelming force is successfully used, the number of competitors drops. A successful program in which you have set a higher standard can cause your competitors to cancel plans to develop competing titles. Stories of success as well as failure become a part of industry legend. Be sure that the industry insiders think that your titles more than adequately cover your subject field; as your reputation grows, your competition will abandon any market you enter.

Reis and Trout in their books concerning marketing liken the process to war. It is indeed similar to a war. Overwhelming force is useful in war and in marketing. Frankly, you must have a killer instinct. If your program is head and shoulders above the competition and is setting sales records, you must devote as much effort as possible to improving the title. As your title reaches the top of the sales reports, it will attract exquisite attention from every competitor. One of the most dangerous times in creating a million-seller is when the title begins to show its strength.

When a title shows that it has potential to be a tremendous best-seller, other publishers will rightfully assume that they can knock off the title. Having a plan for making a ten-times change in your software, you can maintain the strategic initiative. By following the tips concerning USPs and organization, your successful title has been designed around your strengths. Your development strategy defines the war, and the battle is beginning. Whether you have organized the title for ease of use, speed, power, or other USP, channel your effort into your chosen battle.

CHAPTER 11

▷ Negotiating a Publishing Arrangement

As the market begins to treat software as a standard commodity rather than a specialty item, the industry will become more capital intensive. In other words, when computer programs are stocked and sold everywhere (like dog food), better financed companies that can afford to produce more stock and maintain larger lines will control the supply in the software industry.

As a result, a programming company with a single product will probably have difficulty obtaining shelf space. This makes being a one-program company less and less possible. As a practical matter, programmers with only a few titles will need to find publishers that carry hundreds of titles to get their products in the stores.

To find a publisher, you will have to deal with the head of the software publishing department. Every software publisher has an editorial director, publisher, editor in chief, creative director, or other official who sets editorial policy and who selects titles from those submitted by authors for publication. The editorial policy includes the types and number of titles and their retail price. Depending on the organization, the publisher may also create concepts for titles and assign them to authors.

In a typical day, the publishing director participates in every aspect of the software enterprise. If there's a creative meeting, sales meeting, programming meeting, marketing meeting, manufacturing meeting, customer support meeting, advertising meeting, art meeting, or project meeting, the publishing director needs to attend. When not in meetings, the publishing director negotiates contracts, contract extensions, and licensing agreements, and makes strategic long-range plans. Many publishing directors are also lawyers and must spend time looking through those international-treaty-length documents that are sometimes misleadingly called "publishing contracts."

In a typical day, meetings and negotiations take about five hours. Then, reports have to be prepared and a staff supervised. That leaves four hours for taking an average of fourteen calls per day, and returning seven to eight others, in addition to originating five to ten outgoing calls daily. That leaves about sixteen minutes a day to look at unsolicited submissions. However, I can assure you that every submission's cover letter is reviewed, and if there is *any* merit to the concept or if the programmer has developed other successful programs, then the program is reviewed either by the publishing director in person or by a senior member of the programming and publishing staff.

Software is an industry in which innovation, excitement, and newness, or at least the perception of them, are at a premium. Publishers are almost always in great need of new and exciting concepts, and take time over weekends and holidays to "cruise the net" and to go to computer stores to look at what competitors are doing. Every software publisher is looking to set a trend and to find a diamond in the rough, and invests time to discover a great concept or great programmer.

Perhaps one day software publishers will, like book publishers, recruit the few infamous and famous persons who are in the news, or rely on agents to find their new authors. But for now, publishers are eagerly scouring for the next programmer with the imagination to write hits.

As in the book field, the software program's unsolicited submission must immediately attract favorable attention in order to get more than a polite refusal. So, what should be in your solicitation letter to get a publishing director's attention? At least forty or fifty books on the market discuss how to prepare query letters, book proposals, and other materials to present to paper book publishers and agents.

Similar (but not identical) principles apply to dealing with software publishers and electronic agents. One significant difference is that book publishers encourage authors to submit book proposals, but not actually write the book until they've agreed on a contract. This does not apply to electronic publishing with equal force. Sometimes a publisher will hire a programming team to write a program to the publisher's specifications. (Or programmers are hired to make changes to existing programs whose original authors are unavailable.) But most software publishers want submissions of computer programs that are complete and ready to market.

Book publishers sometimes take risks on persons who've never completed a publication, but most insist on some prior publishing or writing to ensure that the person they've advanced royalties to will produce a delivered, salable manuscript. This does not apply with equal force to computer publication. In the computer world, not only does an author have to be creative, but he or she also has to be proficient in completing a debugged, ready-for-market program. A degree in information processing can get someone a job as a junior programmer doing "grunt work" programming in a corporate environment. However, in the commercial publishing world, few programmers are hired without samples of their work. Although some programmer certification courses are now offered, every programmer whom I have ever been involved in hiring, and every programmer who has told me about his or her job interviews, has had to present some sort of actual working program to get the job.

To complete a paper book, the deliverables can be made with a pen and paper. Fixing a paper book that has gone off the rails may require copyediting or bringing in ghosts to clean up a project. But the key point is that all that paper book publishers have to do to "fix" a broken project is change words. Many more things can go wrong in electronic publishing than in paper book publishing. If a computer program doesn't work, it is normally impossible for another programmer to pick up and complete the project.

Delays in paper publishing can cause problems, but delays in preparing a computer program for market may render the computer program totally obsolete because of technology changes. The "operating system" isn't going to change for paper books, and new "printer drivers" won't be needed to use a book, but changes in either of these may delay a software project by months. Can you imagine users waiting to buy a book until after the next miracle chip that's been announced is on the market? Such issues as format are not insurmountable for books, but the transition from disks of varying sizes to CD-ROM and other formats like DVD has huge potential implications for computer programs.

So, there may be significant changes in some business aspects of paper books, but the content and deliverables for the market are stable. A book publisher can plan books on a one-year or even longer cycle, but a computer publisher faces tremendous risks in planning that far ahead. All these factors combine to make selling a computer program to publishers when it's only a concept more difficult.

If you have a completed program, you will of course submit that to a publisher. However, if you have a great concept, a prototype with some of the major functions completed is enough to start negotiations. (Some programmers are reluctant to show their work prior to completion. There is a natural fear that ideas will be stolen. As discussed in Chapter 12, this is such a rare occurrence with legitimate publishers that there is no reason to withhold concepts. The real problem that publishers have is too many good ideas.)

If you wait until you have a finished program before you approach agents or publishers, you may create a program for which there is no market. (For example, to most programmers, writing games is a favorite pastime. Therefore the most frequent submissions publishers receive are games. There are thousands of games looking for publishers. Even if the game makes it to the shelf, the odds are that the game will not earn enough money to earn its keep. The market is so saturated, and games represent such a risk, that beginning programmers would be advised to try anything but a game.) Given that computer programs need to be nearly complete before submission to a publisher, a very good eye for what the public wants is critical. That "eye" or intuition for good topics has meant the difference between long-term success and failure of publishers and programmers alike. Fortunately, event-driven programming and graphical user interfaces, now the rage in the consumer market, allow you to create a prototype pretty quickly using tools like Borland's Delphi or Microsoft Visual Basic. With such tools, you can prepare virtually complete interfaces without the need to do much of the underlying programming.

With a program or prototype in hand, there are several different ways to get a program reviewed by a publisher. But the first question is which publisher? Every director of publishing gets excellent work that he or she cannot use because the program doesn't fit the company's market niche or corporate image. Some publishers send a polite rejection letter stating "that the title does not fit our immediate needs." I have legitimately turned down titles that in themselves were excellent and would do very well for another publisher.

Field work is the best way to find a good fit. The easiest sell is to a publisher that is attempting to maintain a catalog of ten or more programs. Visit a large computer superstore and look for publishers that have a significant amount of shelf space. Then, get a copy of a research report like *PC Data* and look through listings of top publishers in the areas that you feel that your program falls into. These are publishers that you'll solicit.

Getting submissions moved from "unsolicited" to "solicited" is vital to obtaining a publisher for your potential million-seller. There are a number of ways to gain a real review of your program.

OVER THE TRANSOM

Except in the largest companies, "slush pile" submissions will get reviewed. Normally, the review is by a senior person (unlike paper books where junior persons winnow out submissions), and then the program is sent to junior persons for thorough testing and more review.

REFERRAL

Visit the booth of any software publisher during Comdex, E3, or the Consumer Electronics Show, and you will probably be able to meet a senior executive (from some division) of the publisher or the director of publishing. Before making personal contact, see if you can get a catalog or at least a good look at the display. Does your program fit? Publishers frequently announce new programs at shows. Do you like the direction the publisher is taking? If it looks like a good match, ask if they'd be interested in your program. If they are, exchange business cards and ask to whom to send the program for review. Congratulations. You have now moved from an over-the-transom submission to an invited submission — your program will get much more than a cursory review.

Remember in your cover letter to let the publishing director know that "Joe Smith" told you to send your program. One last hint, wait about a week and a half after the show before submitting your program. The flood of mail and calls right after a major show is distracting.

TRADE SHOWS

Rent the smallest possible booth that you can at a major trade show. Better yet, share the cost with another startup company. Hire a professional graphic artist and get an excellent box cover. Wallpaper your booth with your program title(s). If you can afford it, have 5,000 CDs made of your program. A self-executing demonstration is best. The most important trade shows are E3 and Comdex.

SHAREWARE

As noted in Chapter 9, release of your program in the shareware market is an excellent "silent salesperson." As a subset of this, place your program on the web. Publishers are looking.

AGENTS

Another strategy to get your program published is to hire an agent. At present, electronic agents are making relatively few deals. Unlike paper books in which an agent is necessary just to obtain a review of a proposal, most software deals are made directly between the author (or head of the development team) and the publisher, for a number of reasons.

Very few traditional agents can negotiate the technical aspects of computer programming deals although book agents are generally well versed in production details like length, art, style, and market niche for paper books. Most book agents have served apprenticeships as book editors or publishing managers. But if there is a technical computer question, book agents are generally unequipped to discuss them.

One of the few true "electronic" agents is Lloyd Melnick of Octagon Entertainment. Melnick agrees that most publishing deals are for programs that are at least at good alpha stage, rather than proposals. Electronic agents are as buried in submissions as publishers at software companies. Melnick suggests that you have something that will catch the immediate attention of the agent. It's the same as when you deal with software executives — you must catch the attention of the agent at once. Show the agent that you have worked on another successful program and have a track record — better yet would be a slick demonstration of your program.

In the recent past, multimedia development tools have significantly improved, as have "slide show" and demo creation programs. You have a very brief time to make a good impression, so place a great deal of effort into making your demonstration compelling. "A short quick demo is best," according to Melnick.

Melnick lists the following reasons why an agent may be the best way to go with a publisher.

The agent knows whom to contact

Agents are familiar with the publishers that have good track records of sell through. Put in blunter terms, an agent knows which publishers will actually give the project a fair shot. Agents know whether a publisher can get your program in twenty or twenty thousand stores. Because of connections and research, an agent also has an accurate picture of which publishers sell through. Too many companies ship out hundreds of thousands of copies and get about the same number of copies back. That's a waste of effort and a lost opportunity. This knowledge is vital and is among the most important element that the agent brings to the table.

An agent will obtain a serious review of your project

Melnick observes that submissions from agents get more attention from a publisher than over-the-transom submissions. I agree completely. There are a number of reasons that this is true. In particular, publishers know that agents winnow out low-merit programs, so they can assume that submissions from agents are of good quality. Publishers also like having professional agents as buffers between themselves and authors. For the same reason that a lawyer doesn't represent himself or herself, an agent provides a professional perspective and brings knowledge of the industry to the bargaining table.

Agents make intelligent multiple submissions

An agent will go to many good outlets with a title. Melnick will often make inquiries to forty or fifty publishers on a single program. An agent knows how to conduct an "auction" of a good title. An agent's most valuable contribution to the process is probably picking the right publisher for a strong concept. The same title may flop with one publisher but make it to the top of the charts with another.

Agents have relationships that they can draw on

The computer software publishing world is a relatively small one. Agents develop good relationships with publishers. Perhaps their previous dealings can open a door for you, and allow you to draw on goodwill developed in other transactions. Will a publisher take a chance on something that is a bit unusual or offbeat, but with potential? Maybe, but the odds are better if the proposal is championed by someone whom they owe a favor.

Agents will negotiate the best deal

Melnick feels that an agent can get a better deal than an author. Although this can't be verified empirically, I agree that an agent can usually get a better deal than an author because the agent will find the best possible match for the author. The agent's knowledge of the industry will make the negotiations go more smoothly; what's more, the agent knows which of the dozens of terms in a contract are most important to the author.

Agents know what is in demand

Agents speak with decision makers in the computer industry every day. Publishers give chunks of very valuable information to agents about their needs and the industry as a whole. If a proposal has merit, but is missing an important element to make it salable, a good agent will warn the author and get the program improved before submission. Melnick has had a publisher ask for a particular type of title and seen a good fit come across his desk the next day.

Agents have international connections

Software is now a truly international market. Agents have real-world experience with publishers and marketing partners in many areas of the world, particularly in developed markets like Japan, Europe, Australia and New Zealand, and Brazil. Melnick, like many other agents, attends trade shows throughout the world, including European Computer Trade Show, Milia, E3, and Comdex, and will represent your work in all the viable markets. There is a general industry perception that certain markets are not worthwhile to pursue, particularly China. An agent like Melnick knows about the places where great deals with good dollar returns can be made.

An agent will also assist in obtaining the best translators and localization experts possible. Making a computer program that is great in one language as marketable in another is a difficult undertaking.

If you're convinced that an agent is a good idea, how do you pick one? Books on selecting paper book agents provide good advice and are worth reading. Melnick suggests the following questions to ask an agent.

- What experience does the agent have with electronic deals? Many paper book agents now claim to handle electronic media. Melnick states, and I agree, that you don't want to be the first electronic sale that an agent is trying to make. Be sure that your agent does in fact have the qualifications to do an electronic project.

- Are they computer literate, with at least a "power user's" knowledge of computers? Some agents can't even answer questions like "is the program for PC or Mac?"

- What strategic partners do they have? Having the right strategic partners will make or break a program. From publisher to distributor to retailer, using the best is not just desirable, it's necessary to reach a million sales. Melnick has seen programs created by top programmers that featured licensed, well-known cartoon characters and had a launch budget of more than $5 million that failed because they lacked the proper partners.

- Can they provide a list of references? A great agent will provide references from authors and publishers who've had real-life experience with the agent. Check out references carefully.

So, you (or your agent) have found a publisher that's a good fit, and you are ready to submit your program. What can you do to help your program make the final cut? Use the following insight into the publisher's selection process to shape your program and submission letter. If you cover as many of these areas as possible, you'll prove that you are a good partner for the publisher, and more of the publisher's staff will support your program.

Here's what happens to a program that gets the publishing director's initial attention. After the publishing director deems a program appropriate for the publisher, the program must go through a further internal review process before the publisher will begin negotiating with the author. Although the process is different at each company, the general outline is the same and always ends with a "final-cut" meeting at which sales, publishing, marketing, and promotions personnel, together with the CEO or the publisher, decide which titles to acquire.

In order to reach the shelf, several different levels of sales have to be made. The director of publishing must sell the program in house; the sales staff must then sell the program to the publisher's manufacturer's representatives; and the sales staff and manufacturer's reps must sell the program to the buyers at the wholesalers and retailers. Therefore, the best directors of publishing are the ones who excel at selling concepts within their own companies. Find a publishing director who can convince the in-house staff that their titles and lines are a winner, and you'll find a publisher with great placement and sell through.

First, the program is sent for a detailed review, by a programmer or an in-house editorial assistant. The staff making these reviews has specific directions and information concerning the editorial policy of the publisher and the state of the industry. The detailed reviewer will verify that each feature on the author's feature list is implemented as claimed. Programmers often do this work because they are well equipped to review the quality of implementation of concepts. These reviews are usually quite technical, involving the style of programming and engineering. It's not at all unusual for a reviewer to reverse-engineer the program to determine the programming language, third-party libraries, and efficiency of coding used. Attention will also be given to memory utilization, including the system resources used and then, if well designed, freed by the program.

If the program supports any peripherals other than printers, these are also tested. Each feature claimed is verified. For example, if a listed feature is "130 templates," the reviewer will check that there are that many working templates in the program.

Quality is not an issue — it is an assumption. Programs with more than a few bugs won't get a recommendation. The program's ease of use, and potential sources of customer support questions, will be scrutinized. A program designed for children will also get a field review with kids. If a review looks good, the reviewer will also try the program on high-end and low-end systems. Programs that operate on multiple platforms (such as both Mac and Windows) will be run on machines that are high end and low end for each system. After the features are verified, the reviewer makes a subjective judgment about the program's worth.

Anyone doing a review is looking for a unique selling point. What is vital, exciting, different, and therefore marketable about this program? How does it compare to similar programs already on the market? Why should the publishing company commit its resources to the project?

A title that survives initial review also has a slide show or other scripted demonstration created, together with an expanded feature list. These items will be used to present the program to other departments within the software company, and will also be used to create a demonstration program and promotional materials for use at trade shows or other presentations.

Altogether a title that shows promise may spend three or four days of staff time being reviewed. It's easy to tell which submissions are winners. When the reviewer is begging everyone to come to his or her office and see the program, that's a winner. The excitement is contagious, and programs that pass internal review are often on every machine in the company.

The program, demo, and review notes are eventually passed back up the line. Unless the reviewers are enthusiastic, the program is rejected without further review. Otherwise, the publishing director places the program in a priority queue. Many publishers use a four-tiered system for ranking titles that they would like to publish. The categories are as follows:

1. Must do

2. Desirable if space is available

3. Chancy, but worth a try

4. This program is worth publishing if we must compete in a specific category

Software publishers rarely know in advance how many titles they'll publish each year. The market is actually that volatile. Allocations of shelf space change, as do industry trends. Sometimes retailers are looking for lots of products. Other years retail buyers, stung by carrying too many titles, reduce their lists and look for quality. New programs might not get released because a hit program has its shelf space allocated at double or triple facing. Because of this uncertainty, and the fact that computer programs can be released on much shorter cycles than paper books, the decision on releasing titles is a fluid one that may change over the course of a year.

After the publisher creates the priority queue, a joint review by the sales and programming staff takes place. Above all, placement (getting the product in the stores) and then sell through (getting the stores to sell out and reorder) are keys to having a successful publication of a title. The persons who are closest to the front lines are the sales staff. On a day-to-day basis, the sales staff is on the front line and has insight into the fickle tastes of the buyers for retailers. This is where the final cut is made.

There are always a few strong personalities in the software publishing business, but generally, a consensual decision-making approach is taken. The entire team must agree on decisions, and the whole organization must commit to directions to be taken. During final-cut meetings, the director of publishing has to be prepared to discuss each aspect of the titles recommended for publication, including:

- Differentiation — Why is this title special? Why will the wholesalers and retailers add this program into their mix?

- Packaging — Can the program's features be translated and explained to the public? The public and buyers select programs based on their covers. Does the program have a hook that can be described in a few words or an image?

- Competitors — What have similar products' sales records been? Does any other company intend to release a similar title? If so, how does our program compare?

- Promotion — Does the title have any great tie-ins? As computer programs become marketed as commodities rather than specialty items, are any tie-ins available? Is there any independent publicity tie-in? What is the likely response by computer journalist reviewers?

- Other markets — Does the program have possibilities as an OEM or educational title?

- Technical — Are there technical problems or limitations with the program? For example, does the software run only on high-end machines?

- Possible shelf life — Is the title an evergreen, or limited? Are there any hardware limitations or specifications, or is the program able to run on large numbers of machines?

- Tie-ins and add-ons — Does the program have potential for sales of subscriptions, service contracts, or any other products?

- Pricing — Which price point(s) might the program fit?

Your submission to a publisher has the greatest chance of success if you have thought through all these factors and presented the best possible arguments that the director of publishing can use to win the in-house purchase battle.

Congratulations, you've been accepted for publication! If a publisher makes an offer for your program, you must enter into negotiations for a final contract. The most important term is *not* advances, royalty rates, or the rights granted; these issues obscure the only real concern: the actual commitment to distribution and sell through of the program. All too many authors have signed with one publisher rather than another because of a 1 percent difference in royalty rates, only to never see anything but token royalties because of nonexistent marketing.

It is not enough to get a program on the shelf. Actual final sales is the real question to consider. A publisher might talk a good game at the start but not be there in the end. The publisher has a responsibility to influence how the program is displayed in stores to give it a sufficient chance at market. With every sign pointing to a contraction in the number of titles in the marketplace, getting released isn't enough. Being placed in the best stores and in special promotions will be just as important. The publisher's publishing director, sales staff, and marketing staff must combine great programs with great promotions to create a high-volume success.

With this warning, here are the terms that are negotiated between publisher and author in the computer field.

DISTRIBUTION

The key term in any publication contract for computer software is not advance or royalty rate, but rather distribution of the program. The money actually is made on sell through of the programs and reorders, not on the initial purchases. An author must determine the extent of the publisher's ability, rather than intentions, to get *and keep* the program on the shelf.

RIGHTS

Many deals are made for all world rights for the term of the copyright. However, most publishers are willing to narrow the scope of rights and let authors retain markets that the publisher is not actively seeking. This can be made easier by requiring other editions to carry different names and have different feature lists so that they appear to be different programs. Legitimate publishers that have no fixed plans for distribution in Japan, for example, should not object to allowing the programmer to reserve the rights to Japan. Shareware and alternative channels also should be excepted if the author has a legitimate desire to participate in the other channel. Go for a nonexclusive right of publication, giving the publisher specific channels at specific prices. For example, if the publisher wants to sell the program for $99 MSRP, give the publisher the sole rights for any programs under the name selected by the publisher, and for sale between $99 MSRP and $199 MSRP. Try to retain the right to release programs in all the other channels. Legitimate publishers are willing to waive rights that they do not intend to exercise.

LENGTH OF CONTRACT

The length of a contract is an important factor for the author. If a publisher has had a reasonable opportunity to work with a program and develop a market for it, and the results are poor, the publisher should be willing to release the author from the agreement. A publisher wanting to hold on to a program that is not doing well is a publisher in trouble. Successful publishers have good projects and automatically cut the weakest performers. Normally, if a publisher has given it their best, either the publication strategy is wrong or the program is not viable. In baseball, a lifetime .300 hitter, a hitter missing 70 percent of the time, is a candidate for the Hall of Fame. A publisher must have a much higher batting average to stay in business. Nevertheless, sometimes a publisher will strike out despite the best of intentions and efforts. So long as there is a name change, and perhaps a feature change, there is no legitimate reason for a publisher to refuse to release an unsuccessful program from its contract. These clauses are normally phrased as minimum sales commitments, with automatic renewals for additional terms. The best publishers automatically discontinue the lowest-selling titles and are willing to release any rights that they do not have an actual intent to use.

ROYALTY RATE

Royalty rates have stabilized in the range of 7 to 10 percent of the wholesale price. Nevertheless, royalty rates should not be deal killers. A company agreeing to 14 percent royalties, but selling only a tenth the volume of a more aggressive publisher offering 7 percent, is not offering a good deal.

RESERVES

Royalties are paid on accrual of sales, less anticipated returns. An industrywide return rate of 20 percent of sales is common although good publishers should do much less. The parties should have a clear understanding of what types of reserves may be withheld and the means for adjusting discrepancies.

ADD-ON SALES (BOUNCEBACKS)

One of the more valuable points to consider in negotiation are bouncebacks, explained in depth in Chapter 4.

ATTRIBUTION

Thousands or hundreds of thousands of programs in distribution can act as a silent sales force in the same way that shareware distribution can. Putting your name on the product can generate sales for your other work.

ADVANCES

No subject causes more controversy than advances. At one time, following a traditional paper book model, software publishers paid advance royalties. This was particularly true of programs that were commissioned by the publisher. Advances demonstrated the publisher's commitment to the author. However, computer software retailing has changed. In the 1990s retailers demanded that software publishers pay large slotting fees (see Chapter 5 for more information), which changed software publishing to a shelf space, payment-driven market. This added potentially hundreds of thousands of dollars of slotting fees to the costs of packaging and in-house development. Many publishers, faced with spending six figures for shelf space, find it difficult to fund further advances. As a result, publishers now can demonstrate commitment to their authors by obtaining shelf space.

When you negotiate a publishing contract, remember that the overall deal is more important than any of the individual components. Publishers that offer more per copy often deliver far less in total sales. A sample publication contract appears in Appendix 7.

CHAPTER 12

▷ Intellectual Property

Every phase of software development presents legal challenges to protect your intellectual property to the maximum extent possible. Copyrights, patents, trade secrets, contracts, licenses, and "practical," rather than legal, protection exist for software, and combining these for maximum effect can preserve the substantial investment made by computer program developers.

You have different protection needs depending on whether your program is under development, complete but awaiting release, or in release. Computer software companies must also be concerned about employees and independent contractors disclosing or reusing source code or tools.

Unfortunately, in my experience, few people in the computer programming business understand even the basic concepts of intellectual property law. Let's begin with a quick explanation of the differences between each form of protection.

COPYRIGHTS

Copyright law is the only intellectual property law in the United States that specifically addresses computer programs. Copyright is the traditional legal protection for computer software.

When the United States ratified the Berne Convention in 1984, U.S. copyright law became "harmonized" with every major country in the world, resulting in almost uniform protection.

Copyright is automatic. As soon as a computer program is created, it is protected by the copyright laws. No search or registration is required although there are benefits to registration. It is a low-work, ultra low-cost legal protection scheme.

Registration does not require that source code be provided to the copyright office, allowing programmers to retain their source code as a trade secret. Copyright doesn't preclude patenting the same program, nor using restrictive licenses. As a result, almost every commercial program released claims copyright protection.

The copyright code provides two different types of protection against infringement. The first is that the copyright code treats the source code of a computer program as text, and copying of any substantial portion of source code is an infringement. "Substantial" can mean a few lines or a single function. Copyright also protects the "expression" of a computer program. Whether or not the same source code is used, copyright protects the "structure, sequence and organization," also known as "look and feel," from infringement. Therefore, a direct knockoff of a program, or a substantial part of it, is an infringement.

Although there are occasional arrests of bootleggers of copyright materials, copyright holders must take their own enforcement action in most cases. To prove infringement, the copyright holder must show that the infringing party had access to the copyright program since independent creation and reverse engineering are not violations of copyright. In the event of infringement, besides damages for lost profits, the gains made by the infringer are also recoverable.

Although it is the traditional protection for computer programs, copyright is seen as less than satisfactory for any true "revolutions" in software practice. Nevertheless, copyright is generally an effective way of protecting outright theft of computer programs, particularly reprinting or inclusion of the program as a whole. At present, copyright generally lasts at least seventy-five years and may last longer. Even "legacy" programs will probably not require seventy-five years of protection, and thus the term of copyright will almost always be enough to protect several generations of programs using the same copyright data or routines.

TRADE SECRETS

Virtually every computer program relies on intellectual property protection using trade secrets. A trade secret is any business information that is not known to the public and that a business takes appropriate efforts to protect. A trade secret lasts as long as the material is kept confidential. The best known trade secrets are soft drink formulas like Coca-Cola's.

Since computer program source code is generally kept confidential, or is released only with restrictive licenses that retain the trade secret status of the code, most developers use trade secrecy to protect their programs. However, reserve engineering and disassembly are permitted and, in some cases, specifically provided for by state laws. In modern object-oriented programming, it is relatively easy to obtain a great deal of information about a program's operation.

No intellectual property right is so ineptly used as trade secrets. For example, many shrink-wrap software licenses assert that the program is a trade secret, but it can't be. Since the program is offered for sale, it is clearly something that is in the public domain, at least as far as its intended operation reveals. (Of course, a beta that is not available to the public is a legitimate type of trade secret.) The law does not uphold arrangements in which a party labels a horse a cow. If it's a horse, no amount of drafting will make it a cow.

PATENTS

In 1994, the last year for which data is complete, almost five thousand patents were issued for what appeared to be "raw" computer programs, such as internal functions of computers. Although the copyright code has been revised to provide for computer software copyrights, the patent code has not been revised even though calls were made to make specific provisions for computer programs as early as 1965. The law in the United States is horribly unclear. Other industrial countries, like Japan and Australia, have enacted very liberal computer software patent laws.

The holder of a patent achieves an actual monopoly for the length of the patent. Since 1995, U.S. patents last for a maximum of twenty years from the date of first filing, rather than seventeen years from issuance. The United States has harmonized its patent laws with the international community after the 1993 Uruguay round of GATT, and now publishes patent applications (which were previously private until issued) after about eighteen months of consideration.

Once a patent is issued, no other party can practice the invention regardless of independent creation or lack of access. Lack of awareness of the patent is also no defense. Like copyright, it is necessary in almost all cases for patentholders to police the market and take enforcement action in the event of an infringement. Experts in computer software patents do note that large players in the software market keep informed concerning issued patents and take steps to avoid creating programs that violate patents. This makes patent protection more powerful than copyright protection in preventing competitors from entering the market. If granted, a properly drafted software patent can ensure a niche in the marketplace and keep others from the field.

There are many drawbacks in exchange for these rights. The average time to obtain a computer software patent is twenty-eight months, with virtually all patents being finally disposed of within thirty-six months. Substantial expense can be incurred in going through the "Zen like" process of convincing the patent examiner to issue a requested patent. The stakes are also much higher than in copyright. Minor drafting issues can substantially affect the degree of protection that an issued patent gives the holder.

The major concern of patentholders is that they must disclose "the best method" of practicing their invention in order to get a patent. In fact, a lack of full disclosure can invalidate an issued patent. However, almost all issued patents do not include source code although the patent application must include detailed flow charts, or enough information to allow someone "of ordinary skill" to practice the invention. The disclosure cannot be so general that it would take a programmer a year and a half to replicate the program's functions. My experience is that those seeking a software patent usually have to reveal more specific engineering data than they want to, but not at a source-code level. Full disclosure is required because the concept of the patent laws is that the inventor is given a limited-time monopoly, and then the public can use the invention freely after the patent expires.

Since patent applications are now released after filing, but before issuance, any truly revolutionary concepts can't be kept under wraps during the patent application process. This means that if a patent is not granted, the idea has been broadcasted to the industry. On the other hand, there still may be protection of the idea through copyright or other intellectual property law processes.

The bigger question is what exactly can be patented. Lawyers agree that over the past few years it has been easier to get software patents, but it is still difficult to determine if the innovation is patentable. Or more to the point, is it even an innovation? The patent code requires "minimum inventiveness." An application will be rejected if all the elements in the specification of the invention are disclosed in a single prior source. The patent office has a huge library of prior art in thousands of fields of engineering, both from patents and scientific and historical documents. However, computer programming innovations are rarely published and are kept as trade secrets by the programmer. Patent examiners find it quite difficult to verify whether or not there is prior art. Indeed, it's tough for computer programmers themselves to make the same determination for the same reason. Many lawyers and their clients are dubious whether patents that they have obtained will stand scrutiny at trial because of the high probability that given enough time and dollars, both of which are in short supply in the patent office, a determined adversary will find prior art that will invalidate a patent.

The larger problem is that in almost every case the item that the programmer wants to protect is an algorithm. Algorithms are the "recipes" for creating computer programs. Unfortunately, in a world where computer patent law is unclear, one settled issue is that mathematical theories or laws are not patentable. Einstein could not patent the theory of relativity although had he done the necessary work, he could have patented the nuclear bomb, a practical use of his scientific discoveries. On the other hand, a time machine using black holes to propel someone, or at least his or her disassociated subatomic components, to another time, could be patented by someone else even though it requires use of Einstein's theory of relativity.

The tension lies in the fact that most innovations in computer science are, at the core, new or improved algorithms. The U.S. Supreme Court decided two cases illustrating this, again Zen, distinction. In one case, a very useful innovation, a means for manipulating binary-coded decimal numbers in a computer, was held to be a "law of science." On the other hand, a device that cured synthetic rubber by having a computer read the temperature in a rubber curing mold by thermocouple, then solve a mathematical formula to determine if the rubber was cured, was patentable.

The reason that the patent was granted for the concept of using a computer to control the curing time of synthetic rubber is that there was a specific tangible result. One of the hallmarks of patent law is that if the description of the patent discloses changing an item from one state to another, the application describes a patentable invention. The patent application for the manipulation of binary-coded decimal worked only on bits in computer memory registers.

The patent laws are still mired in a world where machines to process cotton from raw to finished are what the statute writers conceived, not electronic general-purpose computers. It is a similar problem for copyright laws designed around books although much worse because there has been no rethinking of the law to accommodate modern inventions, whereas the copyright law has been changed to include computer programs.

Well-established patent law provides that algorithms or other basic scientific discoveries, even if "discovered," are not appropriate subjects of patent protection. Algorithms are automatically considered to be "prior art" that is known to the public and thus not patentable.

The courts have created a mechanism for dealing with computer software patents in the absence of congressional guidance. All computer patents are examined to see if they recite an algorithm. If a patent application includes an algorithm, the patent cannot be granted if the practical effect of the patent would be to prevent others from using the algorithm. Thus a patent will be granted if the algorithm is limited to a specific, useful application.

Patent lawyers are "pleading around" the requirement that a patent not preempt the algorithm by tying the results of the algorithm to specific hardware or display elements. As a clarification to the algorithm rule, the courts have also ruled that a general-purpose computer becomes a special-purpose computer when it is programmed for a specific purpose. Accordingly, the general-purpose computer software that implements an algorithm is not patentable, but the "new machine" that can now do different work is patentable. For example, a patent was granted for a specification that described an algorithm for reading electrocardiograms and then making a recommended diagnosis. The court found that a new "machine" was created, in the same way that someone invents a new mousetrap.

Lawyers all agree that the Patent Office is nevertheless granting patents that are for control of internal processes within the computer and are never specifically shown as output to the users of the computer. A combination of lack of prior art libraries and clever drafting around "algorithm preemption" has made the goal of preempting others from using an algorithm close to a reality. Until the Congress acts, besides being "Zen-like" the subject of computer patents will also have "Alice in Wonderland" qualities.

Software patents are extremely controversial. In fact, there is a general mood that "the emperor doesn't have new clothes." There is a new industry of patent purchasers who comb the patent records for old patents related to computers and the Internet, and then send invitations to everyone in the computer industry to buy a license to use them. In the real world, most of the invitations don't get an RSVP. This is because, in many cases, there is so much prior art that the recipients of the cease and desist letters could defend any patent infringement action brought.

Of course, there are well-known cases, like Stac Corporation against Microsoft, in which the issue was taken to trial, and significant damage awards were granted by the court. Even more important, the Stac decision required a cessation in shipment of infringing goods: Microsoft's flagship Windows operating system and MS-DOS 6.2.

Even if someone receives a cease and desist letter, the odds are that the patentholder would never sue because the potential monetary recovery would be very low in most cases. Nevertheless, patentholders do spend time trying to enforce their patents, especially with large multinational corporate potential licensees. Even more interesting is that most large corporations do not actually pay any significant net patent fees. In most cases, if the patents appear to be somewhat valid, the corporation licenses the patent for a token amount, and then promptly sends a demand to the other side to license one of the corporation's patents. Intellectual property lawyers suggest that developers obtain a portfolio of patents for the express purpose of cross-licensing with other holders of copyrights. It's a "mutual admiration" society in which no one wants to weaken its own position by arguing that someone else's patents are flawed.

Another reason for controversy is that computer programmers take offense at the concept of patenting algorithms, even if drafted artfully. In many cases, early software patents seemed to prevent programmers from using without payment routines that were well known within the art of computer programming. This ambivalence also reaches the boardroom of large corporations, which wonder when a patent that covers a basic building block of computer programs will result in an expensive nuisance suit and, with the state of law being so poor, a significant monetary loss.

Nevertheless, software patents are here to stay, and even given the poor state of law in the United States, overseas venues do have well thought through and developed software patent systems, and developers should make investments in consulting patent counsel to obtain strong patents.

PRACTICAL PROTECTION

As noted in Chapter 9, economic imperatives have prompted end users to make extra, less than authorized copies of software. One variety of "practical" rather than legal protection of software is to price the software for retail sale so that buying more legal copies is as attractive as, or more attractive than, copying.

Opportunities for "practical" copy protection occur during lags in technology. For example, as this chapter is being written, most people don't own CD-ROM writers. If a program occupies a lot of space, a CD can hold the equivalent of several hundred floppy disks worth of content. This type of "copy protection" greatly favors lower-priced producers.

Another form of practical copy protection is the availability of multiple packs of programs with pricing that encourages purchasing rather than copying programs. Since the incremental cost of additional sales, like slotting fees and advertising, are eliminated on multiple-user sales, pricing programs that are going to be used in groups should be based on a formula that encourages purchasing in packs.

Any office application, like spreadsheets, databases, and word processors, that will be used both at home and at work are excellent candidates for multiple pricing. There are great advantages in having the same software used throughout a business and having employees be able to use the same software if they work at home. With telecommuting now becoming institutionalized in the workplace, the cost of providing licensed software to workers who split time between the office and their home is now appearing on corporate balance sheets. Getting software adopted within the industry because deep discounts are available on second and third copies of software will create a significant competitive advantage for software companies providing multiple pricing.

The software industry is making an error in not aggressively pricing multiple-copy purchases since the odds favor that customers will make an extra copy or two anyway. Generally, discounts become available only on unit purchases of twenty or more programs. Like shareware, it's time for another "crazy" idea. Keep in mind that the second and third copies will not require a full set of manuals, but only disks. I anticipate many publishers object to this concept because they feel that this will result in even more copies being made of software. However, I think that this policy, rather than encouraging dishonesty, would increase the number of persons paying for multicopies that they were going to make anyway. There is money on the table, and leaving it is not a great idea.

A discount schedule that will encourage purchases is

Two copies — 125% of one copy (one set of manuals, two sets of disks)

Six copies — 200% of one copy (one set of manuals, six sets of disks)

Twelve copies — 400% of one copy (two sets of manuals, six sets of disks)

The final practical protection of a concept is, paradoxically, releasing the program as quickly as possible. Even with a competitor's greatly accelerated counterdevelopment, a new type of program will require months to produce. Every expert in marketing gives the innovator in a field, so long as it is adept at business, the best chance to achieve identification with a market. Pioneering companies like Xerox may falter from time to time, but with focused management can retake a preeminent place in the market from late-arriving competitors.

Getting a program on the market *always* reduces technological and other unavoidable market risks.

CONTRACTUAL PROVISIONS

Computer entrepreneurs have attempted to fill in the gaps between copyright, patent, trade secret, and trade names by restrictive licenses. Two different series of contracts are used: the first for sale of programs to the public, the other for protecting software prior to release.

In retail sales, the usual strategy was to create a legal fiction of "licensing" software for retail sale, even though it appeared to be an outright sale, and making significant restrictions on the use of the software. A typical shrink-wrap license software agreement included:

- No disassembly of the code

- Limit to making one archival copy

- Acknowledging the fact that unspecified parts of the programs were trade secrets

- Liability limitations

Each restriction was difficult to monitor and enforce. The major issue that concerned lawyers was that after a complete purchase was made by a consumer, they were then confronted with a license agreement that they had not seen. It was obvious that they hadn't seen the license since the license was inside a sealed package. Would a court uphold that nonnegotiated contract of adhesion?

In 1995, a federal court held that the transaction was a complete sale and that the license terms did not apply to the purchaser, who had in reality never seen the terms and couldn't return the software after opening the package and reading the terms since most publishers and retailers had "no refund" policies. A later decision has upheld the concept of a "hidden" license, but only if the user has an unfettered right to make a return. Until the "no return" signs are removed from retailers' walls, the courts will not enforce every clause in a non-negotiated, sight unseen, contract.

Court decisions have not yet addressed whether each term is enforceable. For example, a "no disassembly" of the code clause is in direct violation of several state laws that specifically allow reverse engineering as a trade practice. An old principle of copyright law is that a work that is protected by copyright cannot gain protections that are significantly beyond copyright. This again makes disassembly restrictions questionable.

It is also an open question whether a contract can make something already known to the public a trade secret, for the same reason that a contract can't make a cow a horse. These clauses will probably continue to be used, at least as psychological protection, whether or not courts uphold them.

The most suspect of all the provisions are liability limitations. The law of "products liability" already provides that consumers are entitled to sue in the event that they suffer personal injury. This has again not been extensively litigated because most software-related losses are solely economic, but it is probably a question of the cost of insurance coverage, rather than liability.

Prior to a program's release to the public, contractual restrictions are the only way to keep the program under wraps. The basic documents used are nondisclosure agreements, noncircumvention agreements, and options. Persons in the computer industry are constantly requesting and executing nondisclosure agreements.

Most business discussions can't even begin without nondisclosures. A nondisclosure provides that a party receiving business information will not make a further disclosure of the trade secrets in the disclosure. The Uniform Trade Secrets Act, which governs trade secrets and nondisclosures, has been adopted with minor changes by all states and provides a nationwide basic body of trade secret law. International agreements enforce similar standards. A nondisclosure agreement does not keep anything that is known to the public from being disclosed, nor does it prevent disclosure of information already lawfully known to the party.

The larger the company, the harder it is to obtain a nondisclosure. The reason is that a large organization may be working on the same or a similar concept, without the knowledge of the organization that has executed the nondisclosure. In addition, since most protection for computer programs is through copyright laws, the fact that an organization had access to a program can result in litigation, whether or not justified.

Many large corporations decline to execute nondisclosures or have "kiss of death" agreements in which they demand that persons who want to present concepts to them waive any rights that they might hold. Large organizations also may refuse to review any items other than those that are patented.

Even smaller publishers usually decline to execute nondisclosures when offered computer programs. This is because, in most cases, the nondisclosure does not reflect reality. I have been presented with many proposed nondisclosures that state that a program, which I have already had described in a query letter, is a "trade secret" and that my organization must agree to various conditions to review the program. The program isn't a trade secret; its existence has already been disclosed. An organization can be significantly burdened by executing a nondisclosure in exchange for taking a look at a program that, the odds favor, will not be accepted. In presenting a program to a publisher, the program is subject to copyright, and there are remedies for plagiarism. An example of a very comprehensive nondisclosure agreement is provided in Appendix 4.

What most developers actually want is a noncircumvention agreement, a contract requiring one party to deal with another in regard to a specific type of business. An example of a noncircumvention agreement commonly used outside the computer field is a typical real estate brokerage agreement, in which the owner of the property must pay a commission even if the broker does not make the sale during the listing.

In some cases, publishers will agree, in order to obtain a desired program, to a noncircumvention process in which the publisher will publish the developer's program to the exclusion of others.

TRADE NAMES

Copyright does not extend to short phrases or product names. A good name can be a significant asset to a program. Program names don't do much to sell a program, but can doom a good title to failure. Cute names fail because the customer doesn't know what the program does. For every Where in the World is Carmen San Diego? there are dozens of cute title names that the public did not immediately understand, and did not buy. For example, a program called The Fuzzy Bears Adventures could be anything from a computer adaptation of a story to a teaching math or reading skills program.

The fact that poor names can doom good programs to failure is demonstrated by the fact that some publishers specialize in republishing programs that have failed under other names. I have been involved personally in reviving programs that did not sell when a cute name was used by repackaging the program with a more direct, simple, and descriptive name.

Descriptive names that are not very strong trade names generally are best. A combination of a strong brand name and a generic descriptive name is probably best. For example, if your program-company is "Screaming Ocelot" software, the best name for a spreadsheet would be "The Screaming Ocelot Spreadsheet."

HYBRID PROTECTION

Most computer programs are protected by a combination of copyright, patent, and licensing. Computer programs that are combinations of motion pictures (multimedia) and literary works (the programming) require a combination of patent and copyright protection, with the source code a trade secret and license provisions tidying up the loose ends. Developers must be sensitive to the fact that they may need to patent, trademark, and copyright a program, together with releasing it with a restrictive license.

One of the most complicated issues of law is the relationship between computer program developers, employees, and independent contractors. Computer development firms traditionally are concerned about the knowledge that departing employees take concerning the company's plans and works in progress.

Any employee who does creative work should have a detailed employment agreement in which he or she specifically agrees to a nondisclosure. One of the best clauses to have in an employment contract is that the employee is required to give a copy of your employment agreement to their next employer. The fact that the next employer knows that the employee has knowledge of trade secrets will make all parties more circumspect in their dealings.

Many employers want noncompetition clauses in their agreements. A noncompete limits the type of work that an employee can perform after leaving that job. Any noncompete must be reviewed by a labor lawyer. Amateur drafting of a noncompete usually leads to violating state-imposed limits on the agreements. Californians should note that the state laws are extremely hostile to noncompetition agreements unless the employee is compensated while prevented from working. An example series of employment agreements are contained in Appendix 9.

Another legal trap for the unwary is hiring independent contractors. Many developers hire moonlighters who write contract code after hours from their regular employment. Under the copyright law, an independent contractor holds the copyright in what he or she creates, even if it is written to the design of the contracting party. Unless there is an assignment of copyright to the employer, all the employer receives is a "shop right" to use the code. The independent contractor, as a cocopyright holder, can reuse or resell the code, subject to division of profits with the contracting party. Whenever you use independent contractors, be sure to have an agreement specifically reciting the party's intentions about assignment of rights. In most cases in which an independent contractor writes a program, or parts of a program, for a publisher, the parties intend for the publisher to buy the code. An example buyout is provided in Appendix 5.

Small legal errors can cause severe problems for computer software developers. Regretfully, finding good legal counsel is very difficult. There are a few attorneys who are computer literate, or even experienced in the industry, but in most cases even legal counsel well versed in copyrights, patents, and trademarks will have little knowledge of the intricacies that drive computer software programming and business decisions. Because of this, many software firms use in-house counsel who either know the computer field or can take the time as employees to learn the details of the business.

CHAPTER 13

▷ Predicting the Future

Every software "expert" who writes about the future of computer software lives to be humbled by the inaccuracy of those predictions.

Chief executives of large computer companies tend to have the worst record on predicting the future. In 1977, Ken Olsen (then the chairman of Digital Equipment Corporation), addressing the World Future Society, uttered the immortal words, "There is no reason for any individual to have a computer in their home." The president of IBM once estimated the world market for computers at "two or three." As noted in Chapter 8, the importance of the Internet was missed by everyone in the computer industry.

Having presented these examples of failure to predict the future, I should rest my case and shut my mouth. But there have been several moments in the last decade when being able to predict the industry's future was essential to a software developer's survival. Since it is part of every computer professional's job to make reasonable guesses about the future, I will discharge this duty despite the potential for ignominy.

Bearing in mind that the track record of industry experts who predict the future is poor, I'm willing to go out on a limb to present the following predictions that provide opportunities for mass market software sales.

Many of these predictions are courtesy of one of the fathers of the software industry, Paul Mace. A "glory writer," Mace developed the first undelete program and other tools that software users now take for granted. The Mace Utilities was one of the first packages that "tamed" MS-DOS and PC-DOS, and made error recovery possible. Mace now creates multimedia development tools and is regarded within industry circles as one of the most astute market observers.

OPERATING SYSTEMS WILL BECOME MORE COMPATIBLE

In order to remain viable, the earliest personal computer software developers had to make correct predictions of the future every time the software industry underwent a transition. For example, should the developer concentrate on the PC/MS-DOS market or move into OS/2? (Earlier, the decision was among *several* platforms.)

The emergence of the Internet, which wasn't predicted by anyone within the industry, may be another one of these transition points. Although it sounds prudent to hedge your bets by developing for more than one operating system, in reality, few organizations can afford to devote either their intellectual or financial resources to more than one platform at once. The days of RCA holding patents for all the radio systems are over; only a few of the largest corporations may purchase "insurance" by cross-licensing several promising developments.

Therefore, every developer will focus on either his or her own system or the industry's open system. With Microsoft's Windows dominating the market since the early 1990s, there has been a short period of stability in operating systems. This "Pax Microsofta" is likely to dissolve over time, and developers will again be faced with selecting the operating system that they think will have the largest market share.

This high-stakes poker game continues. If you are determined to develop for more than one platform, remember that it takes at least twice the money and brain power to create code for more than one platform.

Of money and brain power, brain power is the harder to manage. Very rarely can a development team, or two teams working together, create the "same" program for each platform without making significant compromises that make both programs worse. Although in theory, languages like C or C++ allow portable development, in practice "porting" code is an extremely difficult process. RAD tools make creating user interfaces a simple process. However, underlying engines, the software that responds to the user interface, are difficult to reuse. Graphics, fonts, and processing power are sufficiently different among different platforms that even trying to design compatible engines usually results in both programs being much worse than if the programs had been developed separately. The "lowest common denominator" is generally exceedingly low.

The final reason that few developers even consider developing for more than one platform is that the market share of the dominant operating system, at each occasion, has dwarfed the market share of the runner up. Bill Gates refers to this as "positive feedback." The return on investment is so much higher if resources are dedicated to what is or what turns out to be the dominant system. As a result, developers tend to make a decision and implement it at once. This is often a "betting the company" decision.

Of all the predictions that can be made, the simplest is that the future will bring portability of applications and data across all computers. Computer data's major strength is the portability of huge amounts of information efficiently. For institutional users, being able to standardize output as well as applications is essential for the interchange of data. Consumers also find their computers more useful when the applications are standardized. These market forces are now compelling a final battle to make applications and their output universal.

Java and other Internet-based languages have created the first opportunity for true "write once" multiplatform development. HTML and ODBC are the first data interchange systems with the potential to allow information and content providers to develop *once*, for *all* personal or other computers. Although it isn't possible to select which of these systems (or ones under development) will emerge as the standard, a high-powered standard application language for distributive computing and access to databases will emerge.

MANY SOFTWARE PROGRAMS WILL CONTAIN ADVERTISING AND WILL BE DISTRIBUTED AT NO CHARGE, OR AT A NOMINAL CHARGE

The pioneers who developed the Internet search facility Yahoo originally used their university's computer center to host their service. When it could no longer rely on funding from their university, the Yahoo team considered all the possible sources for funding the Yahoo web site. They could either charge users, charge the sites that are mentioned on the service, or go to a broadcast model, where advertisers support the service. Like many other online service providers, Yahoo chose to sell advertising to support their service.

Advertisers like this type of exposure because it is quantifiable. They can obtain statistical data showing the number of impressions and the number of links that their Internet advertising generates. In charging advertisers, Internet pioneers have drawn on precedents established for many other information delivery services. Commercial broadcast television and radio have provided programming free to their audience, all supported by advertising. A beautifully printed magazine like *Cosmopolitan* is sold below the printing cost of the magazine, and many daily newspapers are sold for much less than the cost of the paper and delivery alone. The advertising covers the deficit and provides profit for the publisher, and the computer software market needs advertising dollars to be able to afford to sell software at lower price points.

For a major advertiser, software can be a better buy than a newspaper. Advertisers can include direct response materials in the software that they sponsor. Software represents an item likely to be used again and again by the end user. Software represents an opportunity to obtain numerous impressions with true "top of the mind" awareness. It's very hard to channel surf when the message is being presented on your computer monitor. As the "intelligence" of software increases, the advertising message can be adapted at run time to match the customer. Entrepreneurs in the fields of advertising and software should begin to make plans in earnest for advertiser-supported software.

COMPUTER SOFTWARE WILL BE A MASS MARKET COMMODITY, WITH LOWER PRICES BUT MUCH HIGHER QUALITY. THE COST OF SOFTWARE WILL LESSEN UNTIL IT IS CLOSE TO THE PRICE OF THE PHYSICAL GOODS MAKING UP THE RETAIL PACKAGE

The pressure caused by low-cost software producers, Internet software delivery, and software underwritten by advertisers will result in the continuation of the present trend in which the price of mass market software is dropping.

The physical cost to produce most software programs, even in fairly elaborate packaging, is in the range of $10 to $14. It's normally less. Mass market software can now be packaged for well under a dollar, and in the case of very simply packaged CD-ROM software, less than 60 cents. If software is distributed over the Internet or online services, there is essentially no cost beyond the development and maintaining the Internet site: packaging, production, and distribution become things of the past.

Allowing a reasonable amount for amortization of development costs over mass market sales, the total production cost of a mass market software program, in fairly elaborate packaging, could reach $14 to $20. With profit for the developer and a reasonable markup for the retailer, an efficient market would gravitate to a $40 to $50 price. Lower-cost producers who can profitably sell software at much lower prices will significantly increase their sales and market share.

Once software becomes a true commodity, price competition will result in consumers generally selecting the lower-costing program among programs of acceptable quality. In the same way that most consumers buy drugstore cosmetics, while a few buy department store cosmetics, the software shopper of the future will purchase low-cost software most often, whereas "boutique" software will be sold less frequently and at extremely high prices. After all, the writing implement market consists primarily of disposable pens, but some people still want to write with ultra expensive $7,000 diamond-studded works of art. At whatever price point your software is being sold, or at which you plan to sell your software, you must make contingency plans for lowering the costs of production so that you can lower the street price.

HARDWARE CHIPS WILL MAKE POSSIBLE TRUE INTUITIVE OPERATING SYSTEMS FEATURING VOICE RECOGNITION, HANDWRITING RECOGNITION, AND DATABASE SEARCHING

Insider Rich Levin, one of the pioneers in antiviral software, faults the computer industry with failing the "80-year-old grandmother" test. Levin's octogenarian grandmother can use a toaster and many other appliances, but she can't use a computer.

As computer professionals, we must step back and realistically evaluate the user friendliness of commercial software. Carefully read a well-written computer software manual, and underline each skill that the user must learn and each task that a user must complete in order to operate even a simple program. You will discover that there are far too many in even the most mundane program. One of the best reality checks for developers is to work the support desk for their program from time to time. The intelligence you gain from this will encourage you to simplify your program. Even better, teach a neophyte how to use your program. Just teaching someone the operating system will show you how much an end user needs to learn to use your program. It's too much and too complicated. For example, if a user types "instlal" instead of "install," it should be a simple matter for a program routine to recognize this error and act on the intended input.

The software industry has tried to create voice and handwriting recognition software for decades. Russian handwriting and voice recognition software has surpassed all Western attempts because it uses a holistic approach, trying to make sense of the entirety of the message rather than character-by-character or syllable-by-syllable recognition. This algorithm results in faster and more accurate translation; however, software has progressed as far as it can.

Prior to 486-class processors, computer users could speed up their systems by installing a numeric coprocessor. The speed difference between doing certain mathematical functions in software and hardware favors hardware by more than 1,000 to 1. Therefore, special-purpose hardware with built-in data dictionaries for various languages and writing styles will be necessary to make handwriting and voice recognition possible. These chips will also be programmed to filter out simple mistakes made by users so that everyone will be able to use a computer. These new chips will also provide an interface between voice and query by example and structured query language database technology, allowing users to access databases by voice commands.

Perhaps the next "Microsoft" is being born in a garage by engineers creating a system to design and perfect these new superchips. You should make extravagant efforts to collect intelligence on any breakthroughs in speech recognition, handwriting recognition, and friendly operating systems. The first to incorporate these features will reap great rewards.

HARDWARE STABILITY WILL BE FORCED ON THE MARKET WHETHER OR NOT THE LEADING CHIP MAKERS AND OPERATING SYSTEM VENDORS CONTINUE TO RELEASE NEW VERSIONS OF THEIR PROGRAMS

Everyone who has ever purchased a computer has suffered a case of buyer's remorse within the month, when something more powerful appears at a lower price point.

Christmas 1996 retail sales were below expectations because the new, more powerful Intel brand MMX chip was announced as scheduled for release in January. Consumers waited for the MMX rather than buy anything in the months before the new technology was available. The computer industry and computer retailing magazines for late 1996 and early 1997 reported abysmally bad sales figures for, and declines in the stocks of, computer retailing firms; many insiders blame the less-than-stellar 1996 Christmas sales on the January release date of the new chip.

The software industry is growing, but computer hardware is still a specialty item rather than a commodity item. The majority of new computers are being purchased by those who already own computers and want to upgrade. This fact has kept the computer industry stuck at 30 percent range market penetration.

For computers to become universal items like telephones, the cost will have to drop significantly, and consumers must be assured that their purchases won't become obsolete in a short time. The industry first proposed a dumb terminal priced at about $400, called "a net computer" or "Internet appliance," as an answer to this problem. The dumb terminal was not well received by the public; interestingly, corporate America has turned out to be the market for the dumb terminal.

If a computer configuration could be made that would last for five to ten years and would cost $700 or so in total, the penetration of computers in the marketplace would dramatically increase. The chip and software houses can make even more money than they do at present, by amortizing development costs over several years and increasing the market share of computers from the 30 percent range to 80 or even 90 percent. The advantages of stability so far outweigh the financial return of the present system that the market will force this discipline on the chip and operating system industry, whether or not they are ready for it. Be sure that you can recognize when this stability occurs, and then change your assumptions for length of time required to recover an investment.

COMPUTERS WILL HAVE FEWER PERIPHERALS AND WILL RELY ON THE CENTRAL PROCESSING UNIT FOR MANY FUNCTIONS NOW HANDLED BY PERIPHERALS. ANY PERIPHERALS THAT REMAIN WILL COST MUCH LESS

New computer users are surprised to find out that after buying a computer they need to invest yet more money in peripherals like modems, joysticks, scanners, and printers. Even worse news is the bewildering variety of those peripherals. Is a 28.8-baud modem good enough, or should you pay more for the 57.6, and by the way, are the 57.6s made by this manufacturer compatible with the 57.6s made by that manufacturer? A novice computer user can't be blamed for giving up and deciding to wait until later.

The latest generation of chips, typified by the Intel Brand MMX, eliminate the need for peripherals like telephone modems. With good software, the computer can now handle communications, and all that is needed is a physical connection to the telephone line. Scanning and other tasks will no longer need to have dedicated boards installed. All that will be needed is the physical hardware to scan images. This trend will contribute to significantly lowering the final cost of computer ownership.

Computer software entrepreneurs should assume that end users will have significantly more peripherals and that the software must be able to interact with more scanners, digitizing tablets, and other peripherals. A fierce battle looms for the best software to take advantage of the power of the new chips and that will handle the functions once performed by peripherals.

CENTRALIZATION OF COMPUTER POWER, THAT IS, RETURNING TO MAINFRAMES ACCESSED BY LOW-POWER TERMINALS, WILL INCREASE, PARTICULARLY IN THE GOVERNMENT AND CORPORATE SECTORS

Change is the only constant in big business. Corporations centralize, then decentralize on a regular cycle, imitating the action of a pendulum.

Personal computers once were a revolutionary concept since all computing before them was done by either mainframes or time-share computers. As all workers became "knowledge workers," the freedom and independence that a personal computer offered was prized. Users didn't need the permission of a distant computer administrator to make the changes they wanted. Personal computers became popular because the early killer applications like spreadsheets and databases allowed users to "program" their own machines with macros and other time savers that they created themselves.

However, business exigencies and information processing facts merged to encourage networking of personal computers. According to Metcalfe's law, the "value of a computer network increases exponentially with each Node." Since large corporations have fired entire layers of management, getting information from data warehouses has become critical for operational personnel, resulting in the installation of networks. Even computer sites with just two or three users find networking better than "sneaker nets."

Networks also allow users to leverage their investment in peripherals. For example, instead of buying several lower-capability printers, computer users on a network can buy one high-performance printer and invisibly share that printer.

The "network computer," which was designed to be a low-cost machine for consumers, has instead been adopted by industry. Institutional users see only advantages in using dumb terminals. Software updates don't need to be purchased for and installed at dozens of sites; they're installed just once on the server, and paid for according to the metered use level. All data is available to those with appropriate security clearance. And for the overcontrolling or paranoid, there is complete access to and control of all users' data.

Software entrepreneurs should plan to have their software available in versions that can be used on centrally controlled networks. Programmers who develop software that is presently available only on mainframes should invest in developing versions that can be used on personal computers. This means that employees who use your software at work can buy and use the software they're already accustomed to on their personal machines.

Government legislation or government sponsorship will attempt to force all users to adopt similar file formats and exchange protocols

The computer geniuses who develop the ITAR (International Trade in Arms Regulations) continue to insist that effective computer encryption software is a military weapon like nuclear bombs and that American firms cannot export software containing well-known encryption algorithms. Indeed, an allegedly "computer friendly" federal government is insisting that both domestic and export software contain "backdoors" allowing the government to decode messages. The U.S. government will continue to make people aware of the fact that encryption can ruin the government's day and thereby create a thriving market in security programs. With free advertising like this, how can you go wrong?

The problem with these government restrictions is that computer encryption techniques are well known to any mathematician or computer science student. Effectively unbreakable encryption techniques and source code are available freely, and new ones become available as soon as they are developed. Academic papers that detail and review data security procedures are a totally unregulated item.

No one can stop the flow of knowledge across borders. Even if the United States classified all computer encryption information, anyone with an education in mathematics can create strong codes. As a result, the U.S. government is restricting the uncontrollable.

To make the theater completely absurd, even if everyone uses government-approved software that can be decoded by the government, no legal basis prevents the parties who are exchanging data to encrypt their messages before using the government-approved encryption software. So when the government decodes a scrambled message, it is no better off than before.

Ordinary citizens and businesses have good reasons to want their information to be secure from any third-party examination. A significant market will exist for software that will keep information secure. Perhaps it's a market you should be in.

THE COST OF VIDEO DISPLAYS WILL PLUMMET, RESULTING IN LITTLE DISTINCTION BETWEEN HIGH-DEFINITION TV AND COMPUTER VIDEO

Many academic and corporate researchers have dedicated themselves to creating paper-thin, low-power, extremely inexpensive video displays. The goal is to be able to make the "holo-deck" of Jean-Luc Picard's Starship Enterprise a reality. Futurists like Mace all agree that this development is a matter of engineering, not discovery. After more than twenty-five years of research, it finally appears that "wallpaper" LCDs (and the computing software and hardware to control their displays) will finally reach the market at affordable prices in the next few years. Since the "canvas" will be significantly larger, art and the techniques used to create an illusion of three dimensions onscreen will need to be rewritten to create software programs for the wall-sized displays. A significant market opportunity exists in entertainment software designed to take advantage of the larger displays.

"MIND CONTROL" WILL ENTER THE MARKETPLACE AS AN EFFECTIVE INPUT DEVICE

Paul Mace has been on record predicting that "telepathic modems" will be available, allowing you to don a helmet that will allow your thoughts to be translated as input for a computer. Electronic hobbyists already have experimented successfully with using the strongest of brain waves to activate an on–off switch.

A nascent industry in "brain-controlled" computing will develop into a major force in the market. Once a system is released that allows more than just an "on–off" switch, consumers will flock to this system as one of the few, true innovations. Keeping close watch on developments in this area will pay great dividends.

MASS MARKET SOFTWARE WILL INCLUDE CUSTOM ELEMENTS

The assembly line allowed identical goods to be mass produced and started a revolution in consumer and producer thinking about marketing. The goal became to sell the customer on using a "generic" product rather than a custom-made one. The use of mass production techniques is so ingrained in our world view that persons assume that customization is incompatible with assembly line techniques. However, microcomputers, robots, and lasers have allowed companies like Levi Strauss to make jeans to order on an assembly line.

The combination of computer power and engineering of robots makes accessible all the cost benefits of mass market production for custom-made goods. Software is an ideal candidate for extensive customization for the end user. The key to personalizing software is for the software to include intelligent agents or ferrets that will scan other programs or databases to determine the user's preferences or profile.

There is no practical limit to the extent of customization that a computer program can do itself. With access to the Internet or other electronic communications, remote databases can be searched to obtain yet more information. For example, a mass-produced software program can include an intelligent agent that searches the user's computer and places information such as the user's name and address into the program without intervention by the owner of the software. A checkbook balancing program will call the user's bank and have account information available the first time that the user launches the program.

Futurists in the 1960s envisioned that life around the year 2000 would include more leisure time as automation took over many tasks formerly done manually. For computers to reach their potential as time-saving devices, developers will need to include code in their programs to customize the software to fit the user seamlessly in the background. For example, in the automobile industry, cars now adjust their ride to accommodate street conditions and "remember" power seat settings. The same type of automation and convenience must be added into computer programs. Developers need a long-term strategy to put these changes into effect.

Part IV

▷ Appendixes

APPENDIX 1

▷ Example Retail Sales Agreement

A typical agreement between a developer and a large retailer follows. Formal parts such as "choice of law clauses," "entire agreement," and "indemnification" are omitted.

RETAIL AND RESELLER SALES AGREEMENT

THE VERY LARGE RETAILER, referred to as RETAILER, and THE SOFTWARE DEVELOPER, referred to as DEVELOPER, agree:

1. **Grant of right to sell.** DEVELOPER grants to RETAILER the nonexclusive worldwide right to sell at retail, direct, electronic, and mail order sale of DEVELOPER's programs as from time to time may be ordered by RETAILER, to end users, and to sell the programs to resellers for resale.

2. **Term.** This agreement shall have a term of one year commencing on the date of first receipt by RETAILER of DEVELOPER's product.

3. **Price.** DEVELOPER shall provide all products at its lowest available price and most favorable terms to RETAILER.

4. **Price protection.** If the DEVELOPER's price for any program shall decline, RETAILER shall receive a credit equal to the amount of price decrease for all units of such program in stock or in transit. Such credit may be offset against sums due by RETAILER to DEVELOPER.

5. **Stock balancing.** RETAILER may return, at no charge and for full credit against future invoices, up to 75% of the aggregate dollar volume of RETAILER's purchases of programs from DEVELOPER within six months, which credit may be offset against any sums due by RETAILER to DEVELOPER. At the conclusion of the agreement, RETAILER may return any remaining merchandise to DEVELOPER, freight prepaid, for full credit.

6. **Returns.** RETAILER may right, for full cash credit against the purchase price, any programs which:

   (i) are defective;
   (ii) differ from the stated specifications of the program;
   (iii) are shipped in material variance from the delivery date, packaging, or specifications of the program;
   (iv) materially fail to comply with RETAILER's directions for placement of upc codes, or other vendor logistics requirements.

   RETAILER shall have the right to return for full credit any units of programs which are superseded by new versions of the same program.

7. **Payment terms.** Payment for accepted programs shall be due net 60 days prox from date of receipt of the programs by RETAILER.

8. **Allowance for coop advertising.** DEVELOPER shall pay to RETAILER a sum equal to 3% of the aggregate dollar amount of RETAILER's monthly purchases of programs for:

   (i) basic shelf merchandising;
   (ii) line listings in price lists and catalogs;
   (iii) inclusion of the program in direct marketing efforts.

   Such amounts may be offset from any sums due to RETAILER.

9. **Preferred placement.** During the month of July, 1997 the programs shall be displayed face out in an "end cap" fixture, together with signage according to the attached sketch. [An actual contract would have an attached drawing of the display.] DEVELOPER shall allow RETAILER a $5,000 credit which may be offset against any sums due by RETAILER to DEVELOPER.

10. **Initial order and volume rebates.** DEVELOPER shall allow a 5% rebate on each initial order for a program or a changed or revised version of any

program. In the event that RETAILER sells more than $1,000,000 of DEVELOPER's programs during the term of this agreement, RETAILER shall be entitled to a rebate of 3.5% on all purchases above $1,000,000 and 4.0% on purchases above $2,000,000.

11. **Automatic order/EDI.** DEVELOPER shall receive orders through EDI. Retailer shall maintain a min/max stocking level of 5 units of each sku.

12. **New store setup.** DEVELOPER shall grant a 5% discount off the total purchase price of products ordered for delivery to new store locations.

13. **Samples.** DEVELOPER will provide a reasonable number of samples to RETAILER for evaluation by the main office of RETAILER without charge. Such samples may be retained by RETAILER. DEVELOPER grants to RETAILER a site license for use of any samples within RETAILER's main office.

14. **Incentives and gifts prohibited.** DEVELOPER shall not provide any gifts, compensation, or incentives to any employees or agent of the RETAILERS.

15. **General warranties.** DEVELOPER warrants that:
    (i) goods sold hereunder will conform to their specifications and are fit for the designated uses and are first quality;
    (ii) goods will be free from defects in materials or workmanship;
    (iii) goods are manufactured in compliance with all applicable governmental regulations;
    (iv) goods do not infringe on any patent, trade mark, service mark, mask work, copyright, patent, or other intellectual or proprietary rights of any other parties.

16. **Insurance.** DEVELOPER shall maintain a policy of general liability insurance including products liability coverage in a single-limit amount of $2,000,000 per occurrence. DEVELOPER shall prior to shipment provide a certificate of insurance and shall obtain any endorsements necessary to name RETAILER, its agents and employees as additional insureds. Such certificate shall provide for a minimum 20 days notice of cancellation to RETAILER. In the event of an uncured cancellation, this agreement shall terminate and RETAILER may return all goods on hand to DEVELOPER, freight collect.

17. **Support.** DEVELOPER shall provide customer support to RETAILER's customers via telephone upon terms no less favorable than provided to any other retail customers.

18. **Reimbursement.** In the event that due to the application of any credits, offsets, or rebates provided for in this agreement, the RETAILER is owed funds by DEVELOPER, DEVELOPER shall reimburse RETAILER for the sums due within 15 days.

Formal clauses

_____

_____

_____

_____

_____

Signatures

_____

_____

_____

APPENDIX 2

▷ Library of Congress Mission Statement

By James H. Billington
The Librarian of Congress

MISSION

The Library's mission is to make its resources available and useful to the Congress and the American people and to sustain and preserve a universal collection of knowledge and creativity for future generations.

I.

THE FIRST PRIORITY of the Library of Congress is to make knowledge and creativity available to the United States Congress.

The Congress is the lawmaking body of the United States. As the repository of a universal collection of human knowledge and the creative work of the American people, the Library has the primary mission to make this material available and useful to the lawmakers who are the elected representatives of the American people.

II.

THE SECOND PRIORITY of the Library of Congress is to preserve, secure and sustain for the present and future use of the Congress and the nation a comprehensive record of American history and creativity.

The record of American history and creativity has to be maintained in order to fulfill the mandates both to protect intellectual property rights (the statutory role of the Copyright Office) and to preserve the record of the past for the sake of present and future creativity (the constitutional mandate: "to promote the Progress of Science and useful Arts"). A universal collection of human knowledge [except for technical agriculture and clinical medicine, which are covered by the National Agricultural Library and the National Library of Medicine, respectively].

A universal collection is essential to meet the present and potential future needs of the Congress (the statutory work of the Congressional Research Service) and of the government more broadly (Law Library, Federal Research Division, general reference services).

All other services and activities of the Library of Congress depend on its core mission of maintaining and continuing to stock the world's greatest storehouse of human knowledge and of American memory.

The collections must continue to be no less broad and inclusive than at present because far more knowledge is being generated in more ways, more places and more formats than in the past. The knowledge needs of Congress and government are becoming more complex and extensive than ever before as we enter the information age in a competitive international environment where Americans will increasingly have to rely on better use of knowledge to succeed; and the access needs of Congress, the U.S. government and the thinking and creative public cannot be made hostage to the collection and deaccession policies and priorities of other less comprehensive and less nationally accountable institutions.

III.

THE THIRD PRIORITY of the Library of Congress is to make its collections maximally to (in order of priority)

the Congress;

the U.S. government more broadly;

the thinking and creative public.

The Congress' creation of the Jefferson Building a century ago has enabled the Library in the 20th century to become as fully open in fact as it had always been in theory to the broader federal government and to the general public. It is unprecedented in human history — and a unique American accomplishment — to offer open public access to an institution that is at the same time in many respects the working library of a government and a de facto national library. The unifying purpose of providing all the variegated library services of cataloging, reading rooms, and reference staff is to afford as much access to useful knowledge as possible to each of these three constituencies.

The National Digital Library effort will provide remote electronic access to the most interesting and important documents of American history and culture for local schools, libraries and homes across America.

The unique and ambitious mandate that the Congress has given its library during the past two centuries is a stunningly original expression of a broader American democratic ideal. For a democracy to be dynamic and self-correcting, its governing institutions must be not only continuously accountable to the people but also solidly based on a body of knowledge that is both constantly expanding and equally available to those who legislate and those who elect the legislators.

Equal access to knowledge for both governors and governed, rich and poor, represents an essential minimal form of empowerment in a pluralistic democracy — and has found expression in our system of public libraries and public schools. The Library has been given by the Congress a series of centralized national functions to perform that are essential to the health of these local institutions: setting bibliographic standards, providing subsidized cataloging, storing the records and artifacts of the copyrighted creativity of America, and creating and delivering nationwide reading materials for the blind and physically handicapped.

Congress has now recognized that, in an age where knowledge is increasingly communicated and stored in electronic form, the Library should provide remote access electronically to key materials. For the general public, the Congress has endorsed the creation of a National Digital Library through a private-public partnership that will create high-quality content in electronic form and thereby provide remote access to the most interesting and educationally valuable core of the Library's Americana collections. Schools, libraries, and homes will have access to new and important material in their own localities along with the same freedom readers have always had within public reading rooms to interpret, rearrange, and use the material for their own individual needs.

IV.

THE FOURTH PRIORITY is to add interpretive and educational value to the basic resources of the Library in order to enhance the quality of the creative work and intellectual activity derived from these resources, and to highlight the importance of the Library to the nation's well-being and future progress.

Implicit in the broad and international inclusiveness of the Library's clientele (both here and electronically elsewhere) is another ideal unique to American democracy: the desire to promote the free exchange of ideas no less than of material goods with the outside world.

There are three essential aspects to this mission of quality enhancement that are needed by America and uniquely possible within the Library of Congress:

A greater use by the Congress, government officials, scholars, scientists, and the private sector of the vast special and foreign collections that are unique to the Library and that are underused resources for specialized needs.

A greater use of the Library's Capitol Hill facilities by scholars and creative people at all levels for the kind of interdisciplinary, cross-cultural, multimedia, multilingual, and synthetic writing that is important to congressional deliberation and national policy-making, but inadequately encouraged both in specialized academia and in advocacy-oriented think tanks.

A greater use by the general public through programs that stimulate interest, increase knowledge, and encourage more citizens to use the collections on-site and electronically.

The Library staff must move more of its efforts from inward-looking and process-driven activities to outward-looking service activities focused on knowledge navigation: helping more people find appropriate materials in a swelling sea of unsorted information and doing things with library resources that the Library of Congress can uniquely do. This requires not merely more development and retraining of staff than the Library has previously been able to do, but also facilitating in new ways more extensive and systematic use by researchers of the distinctive materials that only the Library of Congress has. Programs for the general public, such as exhibits or publications, must demonstrate the value of the collections and promote pride and participation in the Library.

THE ENABLING INFRASTRUCTURE

To accomplish its mission the Library must have an efficient and effective infrastructure with four key components:

A. The motivation and mobilization of human resources in all parts and at all levels of the Library.

There are four important elements within this category:

recruiting, assessing, holding accountable and, where merited, recognizing the achievements of the work force on the basis of objective evaluations of skills and performance.

training, developing and, where needed, retooling the work force to perform new functions in new ways.

promoting fairness, equal opportunity, and respect for diversity at all levels and in all parts of the Library.

fostering communication and consultation to promote innovation and increase participation in decision-making and the implementation of change.

B. The provision and delivery of electronic services in order to serve the departments of the Library in the execution of the Library's overall priority missions with speed, quality, and economy.

C. The allocation and use of space and equipment in order to preserve and make accessible the artifactual collections and maximize the efficiency, productivity and well-being of the staff.

D. The operation of modern financial and information systems to facilitate decision-making and ensure accountability.

IMPLICATIONS

All of these priorities and the enabling infrastructure are essential and must receive some level of support if the Library is to be able to raise the money to survive, but they are outlined in order of absolute importance so that, if further cuts have to be made, they can be administered in accordance with these priorities.

A constant effort must be made to reduce or eliminate activities that perpetuate procedure rather than extend service; process must give way to substance. We must rely on less paper and more "walk-around," and devote less attention to past practices and turf protection as we continually reexamine what we should be doing both inside and outside the organization. The objective for the next year or more should be to eliminate functions and activities that may have been desirable in the past but do not support core priorities or do not support them well enough to justify their costs.

APPENDIX 3

▷ Unsolicited Contract Proposal Regulations

The following subpart from the Federal Acquisition Regulations sets forth the procedures for presenting unsolicited contracts.

SUBPART 15.5 UNSOLICITED PROPOSALS

15.500 Scope of subpart

This subpart prescribes policies and procedures for submission, receipt, evaluation, and acceptance of unsolicited proposals. It does not govern the competitive selection of basic research proposals (see 6.102(d)(2)).

15.501 Definitions

Advertising material, as used in this subpart, means material designed to acquaint the Government with a prospective contractor's present products or potential capabilities, or to determine the Government's interest in buying these products.

Commercial item offer means an offer of a commercial item the vendor wishes to see introduced in the Government's supply system as an alternate or replacement for an existing supply item.

Contribution, as used in this subpart, means a concept, suggestion, or idea presented to the Government for its use with no indication that the source intends to devote any further effort to it on the Government's behalf.

Coordinating office, as used in this subpart, means a point of contact established within the agency to coordinate the receipt, evaluation, and disposition of unsolicited proposals.

Technical correspondence, as used in this subpart, means written requests for information regarding Government interest in research areas, submissions of research descriptions, preproposal explorations, and other written technical inquiries.

Unsolicited proposal means a written proposal that is submitted to an agency on the initiative of the submitter for the purpose of obtaining a contract with the Government and which is not in response to a formal or informal request (other than an agency request constituting a publicized general statement of needs).

15.502 Policy

Agencies may accept unsolicited proposals in accordance with 15.507. To award a contract based on an unsolicited proposal without providing for full and open competition requires that appropriate authority exists in subpart 6.3. In this connection, 6.302-1(a)(2)(i) provides special authority for unsolicited research proposals.

15.503 General

(a) Unsolicited proposals are a valuable means for Government agencies to obtain innovative or unique methods or approaches to accomplishing their missions from sources outside the Government.

(b) Advertising material, commercial item offers, contributions, or technical correspondence as defined in 15.501 are not unsolicited proposals.

(c) A valid unsolicited proposal must-

 (1) Be innovative and unique;

 (2) Be independently originated and developed by the offeror;

 (3) Be prepared without Government supervision;

 (4) Include sufficient detail to permit a determination that Government support could be worthwhile and the proposed work could benefit the agency's research and development or other mission responsibilities; and

 (5) Not be an advance proposal for a known agency requirement that can be acquired by competitive methods.

(d) Unsolicited proposals in response to a publicized general statement of agency needs are considered to be independently originated.

(e) Agencies that receive unique and innovative unsolicited proposals not related to their missions may identify for the offeror other agencies whose missions bear a reasonable relationship to the proposal's subject matter.

15.504 Advance guidance

(a) Agencies shall encourage potential offerors to make preliminary contacts with appropriate agency personnel before expending extensive effort on a detailed unsolicited proposal or submitting proprietary data to the Government. These preliminary contacts should include-

(1) Inquiries as to the general need for the type of effort contemplated; and

(2) Contacts with agency technical personnel for the limited purpose of obtaining an understanding of the agency mission and responsibilities relative to the type of effort contemplated.

(b) Agencies shall make available to potential offerors of unsolicited proposals at least the following free written information:

(1) Definition (see 15.501), and content (see 15.505), of an unsolicited proposal acceptable for formal evaluation.

(2) Requirements concerning responsible prospective contractors (see subpart 9.1), and organizational conflicts of interest (see subpart 9.5).

(3) Role of technical correspondence before proposal preparation.

(4) Agency contact points for information regarding advertising, contributions, solicitation mailing lists, and other types of transactions frequently mistaken for unsolicited proposals.

(5) Procedures for submission and evaluation of unsolicited proposals.

(6) Information sources on agency objectives and areas of potential interest.

(7) Instructions for identifying and marking proprietary information so that restrictive legends conform to 15.509.

(c) Agency personnel shall conduct personal contacts without making any agency commitments concerning the acceptance of unsolicited proposals.

15.505 Content of unsolicited proposals

Unsolicited proposals should contain the following information to permit consideration in an objective and timely manner:

(a) Basic information including-

(1) Offeror's name and address and type of organization; e.g., profit, nonprofit, educational, small business;

(2) Names and telephone numbers of technical and business personnel to be contacted for evaluation or negotiation purposes;

(3) Identity of proprietary data to be used only for evaluation purposes;

    (4) Names of other Federal, State, local agencies, or parties receiving the proposal or funding the proposed effort;

    (5) Date of submission; and

    (6) Signature of a person authorized to represent and contractually obligate the offeror.

(b) Technical information including-

    (1) Concise title and abstract (approximately 200 words) of the proposed effort;

    (2) A reasonably complete discussion stating the objectives of the effort or activity, the method of approach and extent of effort to be employed, the nature and extent of the anticipated results, and the manner in which the work will help to support accomplishment of the agency's mission;

    (3) Names and biographical information on the offeror's key personnel who would be involved, including alternates; and

    (4) Type of support needed from the agency; e.g., facilities, equipment, materials, or personnel resources.

(c) Supporting information including-

    (1) Proposed price or total estimated cost for the effort in sufficient detail for meaningful evaluation;

    (2) Period of time for which the proposal is valid (a six month minimum is suggested);

    (3) Type of contract preferred;

    (4) Proposed duration of effort;

    (5) Brief description of the organization, previous experience in the field, and facilities to be used; and

    (6) Required statements, if applicable, about organizational conflicts of interest, security clearances, and environmental impacts.

15.506 Agency procedures

(a) Agencies shall establish procedures, including assurance of accountability, for controlling the receipt, evaluation, and timely disposition of proposals consistent with the requirements of this subpart. The procedures shall include controls on the reproduction and disposition of proposal material, particularly data identified by the offeror as subject to duplication, use, or disclosure restrictions.

(b) Agencies shall establish contact points (see 15.504) to coordinate the receipt and handling of unsolicited proposals. Contact points outside agency contracting offices shall coordinate with qualified contracting personnel.

15.506-1 Receipt and initial review

(a) Before initiating a comprehensive evaluation, the agency contact point shall determine if the unsolicited proposal-

   (1) Contains sufficient technical and cost information;
   (2) Has been approved by a responsible official or other representative authorized to contractually obligate the offeror; and
   (3) Complies with the marking requirements of 15.509.

(b) If the proposal meets these requirements, the contact point shall promptly acknowledge and process the proposal. If it does not, the contact point shall provide the offeror an opportunity to submit the required data.

(c) Agencies are not required to perform comprehensive evaluations of unsolicited proposals not related to their missions. If such proposals are received, the agency contact point shall promptly reply to the offeror, state how the agency interprets the proposal, and why it is not being evaluated.

15.506-2 Evaluation

(a) Comprehensive evaluations shall be coordinated by the agency contact point, who shall attach or imprint on each unsolicited proposal circulated for evaluation the legend required by 15.509(d). When performing a comprehensive evaluation of an unsolicited proposal, evaluators shall consider the following factors, in addition to any others appropriate for the particular proposal:

   (1) Unique and innovative methods, approaches, or concepts demonstrated by the proposal.
   (2) Overall scientific, technical, or socio-economic merits of the proposal.
   (3) Potential contribution of the effort to the agency's specific mission.
   (4) The offeror's capabilities, related experience, facilities, techniques, or unique combinations of these which are integral factors for achieving the proposal objectives.
   (5) The qualifications, capabilities, and experience of the proposed principal investigator, team leader, or key personnel who are critical in achieving the proposal objectives.

(b) The evaluators shall notify the coordinating office of their conclusions and recommendations when the evaluation is completed.

15.507 Contracting methods

(a) A favorable comprehensive evaluation of an unsolicited proposal does not, in itself, justify awarding a contract without providing for full and open competition. Agency contact points shall return an unsolicited proposal to the offeror, citing reasons, when its substance-

    (1) Is available to the Government without restriction from another source;

    (2) Closely resembles a pending competitive acquisition requirement; or

    (3) Does not demonstrate an innovative and unique method, approach, or concept.

(b) The contracting officer may commence negotiation only when-

    (1) The unsolicited proposal has received a favorable comprehensive evaluation;

    (2) The unsolicited proposal is not of the character described in 15.507(a);

    (3) The agency technical office sponsoring the contract supports its recommendation with facts and circumstances that preclude competition, including consideration of the evaluation factors in 15.506-2(a), furnishes the necessary funds, and provides the certification required by 6.303-2(b);

    (4) The contracting officer has complied with the synopsis requirements of subpart 5.2; and

    (5) The contracting officer has executed any justification and obtained any approval or determination and findings that is required by subpart 6.3. (For unsolicited research proposals, see 6.302-1(a)(2)(i). A valid unsolicited proposal for other than research may be accepted only if otherwise permissible under other provisions of subpart 6.3.)

(c) If the unsolicited proposal is acceptable for award without competition, the agency and offeror shall use the proposal as the basis for negotiation.

15.508 Prohibitions

(a) Government personnel shall not use any data, concept, idea, or other part of an unsolicited proposal as the basis, or part of the basis, for a solicitation or in negotiations with any other firm unless the offeror is notified of and agrees to the intended use. However, this prohibition does not preclude using any data, concept, or idea available to the Government from other sources without restriction.

(b) Government personnel shall not disclose restrictively marked information (see 15.509 and 3.104) included in an unsolicited proposal. The disclosure of such information concerning trade secrets, processes, operations, style of work, apparatus, and other matters, except as authorized by law, may result in criminal penalties under 18 U.S.C. 1905.

15.509 Limited use of data

(a) An unsolicited proposal may include data that the offeror does not want disclosed for any purpose other than evaluation. If the offeror wishes to restrict the proposal, the title page must be marked with the following legend:

> USE AND DISCLOSURE OF DATA
> The data in this proposal shall not be disclosed outside the Government and shall not be duplicated, used, or disclosed in whole or in part for any purpose other than to evaluate the proposal; provided, that if a contract is awarded to this offeror as a result of or in connection with the submission of these data, the Government shall have the right to duplicate, use, or disclose the data to the extent provided in the contract. This restriction does not limit the Government's right to use information contained in the data if it is obtainable from another source without restriction. The data subject to this restriction are contained in Sheets _____.

(b) The offeror shall also mark each restricted sheet with the following legend:

> Use or disclosure of proposal data is subject to the restriction on the title page of this Proposal.

(c) The coordinating office shall return to the offeror any unsolicited proposal marked with a legend different from that provided in 15.509(a). The return letter will state that the proposal cannot be considered because it is impracticable for the Government to comply with the legend and that the agency will consider the proposal if it is resubmitted with the proper legend.

(d) The coordinating office shall place a cover sheet on the proposal or clearly mark it as follows, unless the offeror clearly states in writing that no restrictions are imposed on the disclosure or use of the data contained in the proposal:

UNSOLICITED PROPOSAL
USE OF DATA LIMITED

All Government personnel must exercise extreme care to ensure that the information in this proposal is not disclosed to an individual who has not been authorized access to such data in accordance with 3.104, and is not duplicated, used, or disclosed in whole or in part for any purpose other than evaluation of the proposal, without the written permission of the offeror. If a contract is awarded on the basis of this proposal, the terms of the contract shall control disclosure and use.

This notice does not limit the Government's right to use information contained in the proposal if it is obtainable from another source without restriction.

This is a Government notice, and shall not by itself be construed to impose any liability upon the Government or Government personnel for disclosure or use of data contained in this proposal.

(e) The above notice is used solely as a manner of handling unsolicited proposals that will be compatible with this subpart. However, the use of this notice shall not be used to justify the withholding of a record nor to improperly deny the public access to a record where an obligation is imposed on an agency by the Freedom of Information Act, 5 U.S.C. 552, as amended. A prospective offeror should identify trade secrets, commercial or financial information, and privileged or confidential information to the Government (see 15.509(a)).

(f) When an agency receives an unsolicited proposal without any restrictive legend from an educational or nonprofit organization or institution, and an evaluation outside the Government is necessary, the coordinating office shall-

(1) Attach a cover sheet clearly marked with the legend in 15.509(d);
(2) Change the beginning of this legend to read "All Government and non-Government personnel....";
(3) Delete the words "is not disclosed outside the Government and"; and
(4) Require any non-Government evaluator to give a written agreement stating that data in the proposal will not be disclosed to others outside the Government, and to complete the certification required by 3.104-9.

(g) If the proposal is received with the restrictive legend (15.509(a)), the modified cover sheet shall also be used and permission shall be obtained from the offeror before release of the proposal for outside evaluation.

(h) When an agency receives an unsolicited proposal with or without a restrictive legend from other than an educational or nonprofit organization or institution, and evaluation by Government personnel outside the agency or by experts outside of the Government is necessary, written permission must be obtained from the offeror before release of the proposal for evaluation. The coordinating office shall-

(1) Clearly mark the cover sheet with the legend in 15.509(d) or as modified in 15.509(f);

(2) Obtain a written agreement from any non-Government evaluator stating that data in the proposal will not be disclosed to persons outside the Government; and

(3) Obtain the certifications required by 3.104-9 and a listing of all persons authorized access to proprietary information by the activity performing the evaluation.

APPENDIX 4

▷ Comprehensive Non-Disclosure Agreement

TRADE SECRECY

(a) FIRST PARTY acknowledges and agrees that during the term of this agreement FIRST PARTY may learn and obtain information, and may in the future learn and obtain information, related to:

(i) SECOND PARTY, its partners, affiliates, attorneys, accountants, shareholders, officers, directors, employees, underwriters, agents or subsidiaries (collectively the "the Parties"); (ii) other employees of SECOND PARTY; and/or (iii) the business, operations and condition (financial or otherwise) of SECOND PARTY (collectively "Information"). Both during and after the Term, FIRST PARTY agrees to maintain in confidence and not disclose, publish, or otherwise disseminate (or cause or permit to be disclosed, published or otherwise disseminated), by any means, including orally or in writing, to any third party the Information made available to FIRST PARTY directly or indirectly by any of the SECOND PARTY parties. Information includes, but is not limited to, any and all written or electronic research, developments, engineering plans, trade secrets, know-how, inventions, techniques, processes, customer lists, financial data, sales, marketing or merchandising plans, specifications, designs, budgets, schedules, source code, drawings, tapes, notes, works derived from source code, agreements and tangible objects. The foregoing agreement of confidentiality extends to documents, tangible objects and information whether furnished before or after the date of this Agreement. Notwithstanding the foregoing, FIRST PARTY may use the Information made available to them if required to do so by a court or governmental body of competent jurisdiction and then only after written notice to SECOND PARTY given sufficiently in advance of the disclosure of such Information to enable SECOND PARTY to obtain a protective order regarding such Information, or if such Information is in the public domain or is previously published or disseminated by a third party other than pursuant to the provisions of a confidentiality agreement entered with the Company.

(b) FIRST PARTY agrees that it will not, without the prior written consent of SECOND PARTY, use the Information made available to FIRST PARTY for any purpose other than in connection with performance of FIRST PARTY'S obligations to SECOND PARTY and not in any way directly or indirectly detrimental to SECOND PARTY or any other of the SECOND PARTY parties. Without limiting the generality of the foregoing, FIRST PARTY agrees that it will make no copies, photocopies, disk copies, facsimiles or other reproductions of, or discuss any of the Information other than in connection with the performance of this agreement. FIRST PARTY shall maintain at least the same level of security in regard to the Information as it maintains for its own most confidential materials.

(c) Any and all documents or materials containing Information, and all reproductions thereof, shall be and remain the property of SECOND PARTY, shall not be used by FIRST PARTY for any purpose except as permitted hereby, nor will such Information be disseminated to any third party except in connection with the performance of this agreement, and such Information, including **all** reproductions thereof, shall be returned by FIRST PARTY to SECOND PARTY at the earliest of: (i) demand thereof by SECOND PARTY, (ii) accomplishment of the purpose for which they were furnished or created. FIRST PARTY acknowledges that all property right in the Information are owned by SECOND PARTY, and that none of such rights are owned by FIRST PARTY.

APPENDIX 5

▷ Independent Contractor Software Programming Agreement

The agreement which follows is for a developer to obtain outside programming from independent contractors. The agreement covers assignment of the independent contractor's rights in the material created.

SOFTWARE PROGRAMMING AGREEMENT

SOFTWARE DEVELOPMENT COMPANY, referred to as DEVELOPER, and OUTSIDE PROGRAMMER, referred to as PROGRAMMER, agree:

DEVELOPER desires to contract with PROGRAMMER as an independent contractor to create certain computer programming code. The compensation set forth hereunder is the sole and exclusive compensation to be paid to the PROGRAMMER.

DEVELOPER shall be supervised by PROGRAMMER solely as to the result to be accomplished, not as to the means of achieving the result. The relationship between the PROGRAMMER and the DEVELOPER shall be that of an independent contractor's.

PROGRAMMER shall prepare computer source code in the Object Pascal computer language, in a form suitable for compilation by the Borland Delphi compiler system, version 2.01, which will perform the following functions for the Windows operating system, version 3.1 and higher:

Virtual Spin the Bottle- (a full and complete description of the program is inserted here)

PROGRAMMER shall also provide "object" files and executable files, together with example input and output of the program. The program shall be accompanied by a complete manual, which manual shall be sufficient to enable a user who is untrained in the program to operate the program in its intended fashion.

PROGRAMMER warrants that it has the right to convey the programming code, manuals and other items which the PROGRAMMER delivers to the DEVELOPER and will defend the DEVELOPER against any adverse claims related thereto. PROGRAMMER warrants that the program does not infringe on any copyright, patent or other agreement to which PROGRAMMER is a party.

DEVELOPER provides such reasonable consultation with the PROGRAMMER as may be required herein. PROGRAMMER shall provide its own facilities.

PROGRAMMER warrants that the code is workmanlike and has been properly tested in keeping with good software design practice. There is no "malicious" code within the program, such as timing out loops or code to cause the program to cease functioning after a certain date or time.

PROGRAMMER herewith assigns to DEVELOPER all world rights related to the software, including the right to publish the same. For purposes of the copyright code, the PROGRAMMER shall be considered the author; however, upon request of the DEVELOPER the PROGRAMMER will execute any and all documents requested by DEVELOPER to effect total transfer of the rights to the program.

In the event that DEVELOPER alters the program and re-distributes the same, DEVELOPER waives indemnity as to the re-distribution of the code.

Delivery of the final program shall be on or about 1-1-1998. PROGRAMMER shall notify DEVELOPER at the earliest possible time that the delivery schedule may not be met. The parties shall meet and discuss in good faith arrangements to be made including possible revision of the delivery date.

PROGRAMMER may during the performance of this agreement obtain access to confidential and proprietary information of DEVELOPER. DEVELOPER shall generally mark such information as to which it claims that is proprietary as "confidential" or by other clearly recognizable legend. As to such information the PROGRAMMER shall take all reasonable precautions to keep the same in strict confidence. Upon termination of this agreement, all of such information which is embodied in written form shall be returned to DEVELOPER. PROGRAMMER shall reveal such information to its employees only on a strict need to know basis, and shall require that such employees execute written non-disclosure agreements.

The total contract price shall be $5000, to be paid as follows:

1/2 on execution of this agreement, 1/2 on completion

Signatures _____

_____

_____

APPENDIX 6

▷ Corporate Pricing

A corporate pricing schedule follows. For purposes of this example, we will use a hypothetical program, The Virtual Water Cooler, which provides all of the ambiance of the traditional workplace water cooler without employees leaving their desks. This program has an MSRP of $99, a street price of $79, and a standard wholesale price of $55.

1. Bulk purchase of complete programs. Purchaser receives full programs and manuals, including standard end user support.

   10 copies or more: 30% off MSRP [Note: some persons believe that below 100 copies, resellers will provide better pricing and start selling licenses at 100 copies.]

   100 copies or more: 50% off MSRP

   250 copies or more: 65% off MSRP

2. Purchase of masters only, network use. Purchaser will be responsible for internal dissemination of the program and manuals, if any, desired. Purchaser will implement a policy requiring primary support through in-house support teams. Purchaser must designate no more than three individuals as eligible for support per 200 copies purchased.

   Minimum purchase, 500 users: 70% off MSRP (3 complete manuals and disk sets).

   1,000 users: 72.5% off MSRP (6 complete manuals and disk sets).

   More than 1,000 users: 70% off MSRP (9 complete manuals and disk sets).

APPENDIX 7

▷ Example Publishing Agreement

The exclusive publishing agreement which follows is a "middle of the road" agreement that is not wildly pro-publisher or pro-author. A non-exclusive agreement might have many different allocations of rights. At the conclusion of the exclusive agreement an example of a non-exclusive agreement shows some rights which may be withheld by an author.

PUBLICATION AGREEMENT

COMPUTER SOFTWARE PUBLISHER, referred to as PUBLISHER, and COMPUTER SOFTWARE DEVELOPER, referred to as AUTHOR, agree:

1. Author is the owner and developer of a computer program for the MS Windows operating system known as "Virtual Kick the Can," referred to as the "program." [An actual contract would refer to a detailed specification.]

2. The AUTHOR grants to the PUBLISHER, the exclusive right to publish the program, under such names as PUBLISHER may determine, for a territory consisting of the entire world, including the right to exploit the program in all forms of merchandising and commercial use known and to be known in the future for a term of the copyright and renewals, if any, of the program. PUBLISHER shall control the promotion, marketing, price, trade names, trade marks, sales and distribution of the program. PUBLISHER

shall use its best efforts to promote sale of the program; however, PUB-
LISHER may use its business discretion in making determinations as to
means of exploiting the program. However, PUBLISHER can not guarantee any specific level of sales or commercial acceptance of the program. All
trade names and trade dress developed by PUBLISHER shall be the sole
property of PUBLISHER. Nevertheless, this agreement shall terminate and
all rights shall revert to AUTHOR if the program has not been actively marketed by the PUBLISHER within a period of one year, and AUTHOR
requests that PUBLISHER put the program in print, and the PUBLISHER
fails to do so within 180 days of the request.

3. The AUTHOR shall provide a complete and accurate vita. PUBLISHER
   may use such information and the name and image of AUTHOR in connection with the publication of the program.

4. PUBLISHER will pay AUTHOR a royalty calculated as follows:

   7% of net receipts (as defined below) up to $250,000

   8% of net receipts (as defined below) up to $1,000,000

   9% of net receipts (as defined below) above $1,000,000

   Net receipts shall be defined as PUBLISHER's net receipts from sales
   or licensing of the program, calculated upon accrual according to generally
   accepted accounting principles with full accounting reserves. If the PRO-
   GRAM is bundled or packaged with another product not subject to this
   Agreement, royalties shall be allocated based on the original MSRP of each
   software product comprising the bundle and payments shall be made pro
   rata upon the portion of PUBLISHER's net receipts from sales or licensing
   of the bundles program upon accrual according to generally accepted
   accounting principles with full accounting reserves. Royalties shall be
   accounted for and paid within 60 days of the end of each calendar quarter.
   PUBLISHER shall have the right of set off any sums due by AUTHOR to
   PUBLISHER for any reason from royalties. AUTHOR, and AUTHOR's
   representatives shall have the right to conduct audits of PUBLISHER's relevant records and accounts related to this agreement upon reasonable
   notice.

5. In the event of program anomalies arising due to the fault of AUTHOR,
   the AUTHOR shall promptly correct the anomalies. In the event that
   AUTHOR fails to correct the anomalies, PUBLISHER shall have the

corrections completed in a reasonable fashion and shall be entitled to reimbursement by AUTHOR for the reasonable cost of such corrections. PUBLISHER shall provide support to end users at its expense, and AUTHOR will reasonably cooperate with PUBLISHER in addressing customer support questions.

6. AUTHOR shall provide source code including libraries and tool box functions to PUBLISHER prior to release and will provide PUBLISHER with any further, improved or altered source code in the event of any revisions or improvements to the program. Such source code shall be retained in confidence by PUBLISHER and shall only be consulted in the event that program anomalies must be corrected and AUTHOR is unable to do so.

7. In the event that AUTHOR improves the program AUTHOR shall promptly provide the improvements to PUBLISHER together with source code as is provided in paragraph 5. However, nothing herein shall require the AUTHOR to make new or improved versions of the program except for the correction of anomalies provided in paragraph 5.

8. PUBLISHER shall include a copyright notice in a form required by applicable law on all copies of the program and a notation that the program is licensed from AUTHOR. PUBLISHER shall promptly cause a registration of the claim of copyright in the program upon publication at its expense.

9. PUBLISHER shall include a limitation of warranty and proprietary "shrink wrap license" in a form customarily used for similar software in the program.

10. Each party represents that it has the full power and authority to enter into the obligation set forth in this agreement, and that it has not entered into any other agreement that would render it incapable of satisfactorily performing its obligations under this agreement or would place it in a position in conflict with respect to its obligations under this agreement.

11. AUTHOR shall indemnify and hold PUBLISHER harmless from any and all claims related to a breach of any representation herein by AUTHOR or due to AUTHOR's performance hereunder. PUBLISHER shall have the right, in the event of a claim to either defend the claim through its own counsel or settle the same on terms which it may deem to be advisable, or, with prior written approval of PUBLISHER, the AUTHOR may defend and settle the claim. In the event that the PUBLISHER carries advertising injury/defamation liability insurance coverages, the PUBLISHER shall at

its expense obtain endorsement of AUTHOR as an insured upon the policy. However, the PUBLISHER shall not be required to obtain advertising injury/defamation liability insurance and shall have total and complete discretion as to whether to obtain such coverage.

12. PUBLISHER shall hold and indemnify AUTHOR harmless from any and all claims related to PUBLISHER's performance from third parties.

13. AUTHOR shall execute any documents reasonably requested by PUBLISHER to effect rights granted herein.

14. [A non-disclosure and secrecy agreement similar to that included in this appendix would be added in this paragraph in an actual agreement.]

15. AUTHOR represents that there are no time outs or malicious code contained in the program. "Time out" refers to any computer or hardware routine which disables the program unless codes are entered into the computer. "Malicious code" refers to any code which may disable the program or system or delete the program or its products after the passage of time or other events. This representation does not include any inadvertent or negligent endless loops or time outs.

16. This agreement is solely for publication by PUBLISHER of AUTHOR's program and does not create a partnership, agency or joint venture. The parties to this agreement are independent contractors. Neither party nor their employees or agents has the authority to bind or commit the other party in any way except for the PUBLISHER's rights set forth herein.

17. The parties agree that this agreement is the complete and exclusive state of agreement and supersedes all proposals and agreements, oral or written, relating to the subject matter of this agreement. This agreement shall be binding upon the successors, assigns and privies of each party hereto.

18. [Additional clauses such as choice of law, arbitration, agent's commission, and non-waiver frequently appear in these types of agreements.]

Signatures _____

_____

_____

Alternative clause regarding rights

2. The AUTHOR grants to the PUBLISHER, the non-exclusive right to publish the program, under such names as PUBLISHER may determine, for a territory consisting of the entire world, including the right to exploit the program in all forms of merchandising and commercial use known and to be known in the future for a term of the copyright and renewals, if any, of the program, as follows:

   (i) the PUBLISHER shall have the sole and exclusive right to editions of the program which have a manufacturer's suggested retail price of $49.99 or higher;

   (ii) the PUBLISHER shall have the sole and exclusive right to editions of the program which have a manufacturer's suggested retail price of $9.99 to $49.99, provided that at the present time that the PUBLISHER does not intend to publish an edition.

PUBLISHER shall control the promotion, marketing, price, trade names, trade marks, sales and distribution of the program. PUBLISHER shall use its best efforts to promote sale of the program; however, PUBLISHER may use its business discretion in making determinations as to means of exploiting the program. However, PUBLISHER can not guarantee any specific level of sales or commercial acceptance of the program. All trade names and trade dress developed by PUBLISHER shall be the sole property of PUBLISHER. Nevertheless, this agreement shall terminate and all rights shall revert to AUTHOR if the program has not been actively marketed by the PUBLISHER within a period of one year, and AUTHOR requests that PUBLISHER put the program in print, and the PUBLISHER fails to do so within 180 days of the request.

APPENDIX 8

▷ OEM Distribution Agreement

An OEM agreement, drafted to be as fair as possible to both sides, follows. A significant portion of the agreement covers keeping the master used for duplication secure.

OEM DISTRIBUTION LICENSE

EXAMPLE MANUFACTURER, referred to as OEM, and EXAMPLE DEVELOPER, referred to as AUTHOR, agree:

1. AUTHOR is the author of a computer program entitled Virtual Pencil Sharpener. AUTHOR is the holder of the copyright, trade name and other intellectual property rights related to Virtual Pencil Sharpener, version number 3.44, referred to herein as the "program". [An actual contract would have a detailed specification for the product included in this paragraph.]

2. AUTHOR herewith grants the non-exclusive right to OEM to duplicate and create copies of the program under the terms and conditions set forth herein. The term of this license shall be five years, unless terminated for material breach. OEM shall place appropriate proprietary, copyright and license terms as customarily used within the trade.

3. AUTHOR grants to OEM a non-exclusive license to use the trade name and trademarks related to the program on its packaging and advertising during the term of this agreement. OEM shall use such trade names in accordance with AUTHOR's guidelines for the use of the same, including artistic and legal requirements.

4. AUTHOR shall provide to OEM a master of the program and camera ready manual for the program on or before March 1, 1999. AUTHOR warrants that the programs are merchantable and fit for their intended purpose. In the event of program anomalies arising due to the fault of AUTHOR, the AUTHOR shall promptly correct the anomalies.

5. OEM shall provide support to end users at its expense, and AUTHOR will reasonably cooperate with PUBLISHER in addressing customer support questions. OEM shall maintain accurate records regarding all correspondence or contract from end users and AUTHOR shall have reasonable access to such information. In the event that such information is in computer format, AUTHOR shall be provided with access to the data in interchangeable format.

6. OEM may exactly duplicate the program and package for the programs for sale together with OEM's Parallel Port Writing Utensil sharpening hardware. OEM may not offer the program for sale alone. OEM agrees to use quality materials in the duplication. AUTHOR shall have the right to examine completed product. OEM shall have the right to make, at no charge, no more than 25 copies for review, in house and demonstration use.

7. In the event that AUTHOR discovers any program anomalies AUTHOR shall provide OEM with a revised version of the program, and OEM shall henceforward use the revised version. In the event that AUTHOR revises or improves documentation for the program, OEM shall either use the revised documentation henceforward, or shall include the revisions in an on-disk file.

8. OEM shall provide AUTHOR with periodic briefings as to changes in the product lines in which the program is bundled, and the parties shall reasonably cooperate in coordination of the releases of their respective products.

9. AUTHOR represents and warrants that AUTHOR is authorized to enter into this agreement, and indemnifies OEM against any claims of copyright infringement, related to the program.

10. In the event that AUTHOR releases any interim fix or revised versions of the program to any other customer, AUTHOR shall provide notice to OEM of the new version. OEM shall have the option to license the new software under the same terms and conditions herein. Nothing in this paragraph shall alter the requirement that the OEM change versions when AUTHOR releases a version to correct an anomaly. OEM shall examine all

master disks for viruses and malicious code, consistent with the best practices within the industry. OEM shall at all times maintain the integrity and security of the master disk to prevent the possible contamination of the disks with viruses or malicious code. Due to the potential for severe harm to the reputation of AUTHOR, this duty shall be specifically enforceable, and OEM agrees to indemnify AUTHOR for any losses caused by any corruption of the data which AUTHOR originally delivered to OEM.

11. AUTHOR shall receive from OEM a royalty of $0.30 (thirty cents) per unit of the product sold which includes the licensed software. OEM shall maintain accurate records of the number of programs duplicated in accordance with generally accepted accounting principles. OEM shall provide a statement of sales no later than 30 days after the end of each calendar quarter, together with payment for sales made.

12. This agreement is personal to the parties and the rights or performance, or both, may not be assigned without the consent of the other party.

13. Upon termination of this agreement for any reason, OEM shall return to AUTHOR all original master copies of the program and any technical support materials. OEM shall provide an affidavit of compliance with this section upon the request of AUTHOR.

14. [A complete non-disclosure agreement similar to that provided in Appendix 4 would be included here.]

Formal parts

_____

_____

_____

_____

_____

Signatures

_____

_____

_____

APPENDIX 9

▷ Employment
   Agreements

An example employment agreement for a technical employee follows.

EMPLOYMENT AGREEMENT

LARGE COMPUTER COMPANY, referred to as EMPLOYER, and , referred to as EMPLOYEE, agree:

1. EMPLOYEE is engaged to act as Chief Programmer for EMPLOYER, beginning on 11-15-97. [A position description with details as to the duties and authority of the employee would appear here.]

2. EMPLOYEE shall receive a salary of $5,000 (Five Thousand Dollars) per month, subject to attendance and leave policies as adopted from time to time by EMPLOYER.

3. [A trade secrecy clause similar to that used in Appendix 4 would be added here.]

4. [Only to be used in states which permit non-competition agreements] specific EMPLOYEE shall for a period of @126 months after termination of not accept employment with the following firms:

[A reasonable list of prohibited employers would appear here. State laws vary considerably, but in general the broader the list, the less likely that it will be enforced. For example, forbidding the person from doing any computer programming unless they are paid during the period of the non-compete will probably not be enforced anywhere.]

4. EMPLOYEE agrees that the duties herein shall be full time. EMPLOYEE shall not engage in other business ventures or employment without the prior approval of EMPLOYER. [Please note that a few states will not enforce the no "moonlighting" clause.] EMPLOYEE agrees to promptly disclose to EMPLOYER any inventions or processes discovered by the EMPLOYEE which are made at the behest or in connection with the duties of employee, or which are reasonably related to the business of EMPLOYER during the term of employment, and shall assign all rights in said inventions or processes to EMPLOYER. EMPLOYEE shall execute any documents reasonably requested by EMPLOYER for patents or other legal steps which EMPLOYER may desire to perfect its rights in the inventions.

5. EMPLOYER may terminate this agreement upon 30 days notice to the EMPLOYEE.

6. Any disputes under this agreement, including those relating to non-competition, shall be submitted to arbitration with a single arbitrator under the rules of the American Arbitration Association. Any ruling made by the arbitrators shall be final and may be entered as a judgment in any court of competent jurisdiction.

7. As to those items not specified herein, the relationship between the parties shall be governed by the general employment manual, dated 2-1-97, and any additions and replacements thereto.

8. In the event of termination of this agreement for any reason, EMPLOYEE shall notify any future employers of the non-disclosure and non-competition agreements contained herein for a period of two years from termination.

▷ Glossary

Affinity product

A product that is related to another and shares the same customers. For example, computer printer ribbons are affinity products to computer printers. Business credit cards like American Express are affinity products to travel reservations software.

Bounceback

An offer made inside a retail package for additional programs, add-ons to the program sold, or other products.

Channel

One of the industries that distributes software. Retail, shareware, catalog, and the Internet are examples of separate channels.

Channel conflict

Sales from one channel interfering with another. Channel conflict is important only if the channels have different profit margins, whereupon the lower profit product displaces the higher-priced product.

Contract of adhesion

Contracts in which, because of inequality of bargaining power, the less-moneyed party simply signs the preprinted, onerous contract. The law disfavors these contracts.

Data warehouse

A transactional computer system containing all an organization's raw data. The data is "warehoused" like other items of inventory and is accessed by remote users, frequently by using personal computers.

Delisted
Removed from inventory at retailers with no further orders; discontinued.

Dump bin
A cardboard box, child's playpen, or other enclosure that holds assorted products all priced identically.

DVD
Digital Video Disk. An improved compact disk introduced in 1996 which can hold eight times what present computer CD-ROMs can. Created so a full length movie in full resolution can be stored on a single disk, which present CD cannot.

E-mail
Electronic messages sent through the Internet.

End cap
Retail space at the end of an aisle; this is a preferred location for sales.

Engine
A program capable of performing similar functions with different sets of data and input. A classic type of software engine is a general-purpose database program. Also used to describe the code underlying the user interface.

Facing
A slot in a retail store.

FAQ
Acronym for frequently asked questions. A listing of the most common questions along with their answers. Since the same questions tend to be asked again and again, a well-crafted FAQ will save your users effort when they want to get help on your programs. A good FAQ generally can cover 80 to 90 percent of user inquiries. FAQs are often included in manuals, posted on web sites, and available via "fax back."

Front end
The user interface to an application. Composed of the input, output, display, and help systems, the front end is the part seen and interacted with by users. The underlying code (engine), whether on the user's computer or elsewhere, performs the

work based on the input collected from the user by the front end. RADs are superb for developing elegant front ends.

FTP

File Transfer Protocol as used on the Internet. "FTP" is used as a verb to describe the process of transferring a file between computers.

GUI

Acronym for graphical user interface. "Invented" by Xerox, brought to the mass market by Apple, and perfected as a market force by Microsoft.

HTML

Acronym for hypertext markup language. A series of standards and near standards that were created by CERN to allow nuclear physicists to interchange information. Now used as the standard for interchange over the World Wide Web.

Internet ticker

A program that collects news and other items of interest from the Internet and then displays them. A more technical description would be intelligent agent. This type of software is programmed by the user and then retrieves information matching the user's interest. For example, an Internet ticker may track certain sports teams, businesses, and hobbies, and search the Internet for items fitting the given search parameters.

ISP

Acronym for Internet service provider. An organization such as America Online or Netcom that provides access to the Internet for subscribers. This may include, besides access to the Internet, proprietary content, web page hosting services, and copyright content such as newsfeeds.

Killer application

A computer program, or genre of them, that is so useful it convinces persons to buy computers who, before the existence of the killer application, were unwilling to do so. Spreadsheets are credited as having been the killer application for early personal computers, and desktop publishing for the Macintosh line. "Killer app" is also used to describe a "perfect" application that is so well engineered it preempts a field. Almost every attempt to create a new killer application fails.

LAN

Acronym for local area network. A series of computers connected in either peer-to-peer, or peer-to-server, relationships.

Legacy system

Old mainframe programs that were developed many years ago; often contains data from large corporations.

MDF

Acronym for market development funds. An allowance, usually deducted from invoice, given to a retailer or wholesaler to advertise the product or to give the product preferred placement. Also referred to as coop.

MIS

Acronym for management of information systems. Title applied to the director of computers for a large institution; also used to refer to corporate computer departments generally.

MSRP

Acronym for manufacturers suggested retail price. A theoretical price for goods that the manufacturer sets in an effort to place the software in a particular price range.

ODBC

Acronym for open database connectivity. A standard for interchange among different databases. Programs that support ODBC can interchange data without regard to the original input's format and database driver.

OEM

Acronym for original equipment manufacturer. An organization that creates computer hardware for its own or other components; usually also includes software. For example, a computer store that builds custom computers from parts in inventory, and bundles operating systems, printer drivers, and so on onto those computers, is an OEM.

Oldenware

An old version of a program, or a program that has been discontinued from front-line sales; also refers to shareware created out of older versions of retail programs.

One way

Software that cannot be returned unless it is defective.

Porting

Converting a program from one computer system to another. This can be accomplished by recoding entirely, using conversion tools, or if the programming environment supports it, recompiling with minor coding changes.

Productivity

Software designed to perform specific tasks other than those related to the computer itself, and other than games and programming tools. Productivity includes word processors, desktop publishers, and spreadsheets.

RAD

Acronym for rapid application development tool; a program that allows object-oriented programming using visual tools. The most popular RADs are Delphi by Borland and Visual Basic by Microsoft.

Real estate

As used in computer software retailing, "real estate" means control of shelf space at retailers.

Returns

Software that is not sold and is required to be accepted for credit when the retailer returns it to the distributor. In some cases, software that has not sold may be kept by the retailer but marked down in price to sell as remainders, in which case, the manufacturer must give a credit to the retailer for the markdown.

Sell through

The rate at which product shipped to retailers sells to end users, commonly calculated in units per store per month. Sell through can be affected by program acceptance and logistical lapses by retailers. Sell through can be very poor if the public isn't interested in the product or if the retailers leave the product in the back room or central warehouse.

Shelf talker

A sign on a shelf promoting goods, excluding normal price labeling.

Shrink

Used in retailing to describe losses due to theft or vandalism. Shrink is measured as the difference between quantities received and inventory, less sales and returns.

SI

Systems Integrator. A consultant who assembles completed systems for a customer, including all hardware and software, rather than a retailer who sells discrete pieces.

SKU

A retailing unit for a given program. For example, if you sell your C compiler for kids as both a disk-based product and a CD, each particular edition is considered a separate SKU.

Slotting fee

A charge levied by a retailer in exchange for shelf space. These nonrefundable fees are required by many retailers in exchange for the opportunity to sell to them. Upon paying the slotting fee, the distributor is entitled to have its products displayed at retail for an agreed period. A slotting fee agreement may also include having the product displayed in a particular place or in a preferred manner — for example, face rather than spine out.

Sneaker net

A series of computers that are not connected and among which data is exchanged by carrying floppy disks between the computers that need the data.

Stock balancing

The right to return product that didn't sell in exchange for other product. The retailer keeps the same commitment in terms of the number of facings or SKUs, but shifts the product mix.

Street price

The actual price that a program is sold at by a retailer, in almost every case at a discount from the MSRP.

String (literals)

Text that appears in programs that is "hard coded." For example, if a program has a dialog box that states "Copyright 1996 Example Developers," Copyright 1996 Example Developers is a string.

Stub (stubbed out)

During development, if a menu or other access point is created in a program but is not ready to work, the menu is connected to a stub, usually a message along the lines of "this feature is not yet implemented."

Time share

Computer network system in which many remote terminals share the processing capability of a large centralized computer. Although the time is "shared" between the computers, the output appears to the user to be instant, or nearly instant.

Upsales

A type of bounceback in which an offer is made within a program for a deluxe version of the same program.

VAR

Value Added Retailer. A retailer who provides products or services to create a "turn key" solution for a customer. For example, a VAR may provide custom programming in addition to all of the necessary hardware and operating software.

Variable

A value in a program that can be declared and changed (as opposed to a literal string, or constant value).

Vertical market

A targeted product designed for a small, specialized market. Vertical market programs are usually specialized applications of more generalized programs. Vertical markets are almost always too small for mass market software.

▷ Annotated Bibliography

There are dozens and dozens of books on my shelf. I voraciously read anything about retailing and software. Here are some excellent suggestions for study.

Barker, Joel Arthur. *Paradigms: The Business of Discovering the Future.* New York: HarperCollins Publishers, Inc., 1992. An excellent view of the future of business in the long term.

Brooks, Jr., Frederick P. *The Mythical Man-Month.* New York: Addison-Wesley Publishers Ltd., 1995. A classic work on the software development process.

Cady, Dorothy. *Bullet Proof Documentation: Creating Quality Through Testing.* New York: McGraw-Hill, Inc., 1996. Documentation is usually the weakest part of programming projects. This book combines a quality control and documentation process.

Carroll, Paul. *Big Blues: The Unmaking of IBM.* New York: Random House, Inc., 1994. A leading journalist explains the undoing of IBM.

Cohen, Herb. *You Can Negotiate Anything.* New York: Bantam Books, 1980. Although negotiation is not a formal topic in this book, understanding negotiation as a discipline is a necessary part of being in business. This book is a great start.

Creech, Bill. *The Five Pillars of TQM: How to Make Total Quality Management Work for You.* New York: Penguin Books USA Inc., 1995. Total quality management can be applied to software development, and this is one of the better guides to the topic.

Cusumano, Michael A. and Richard W. Selby. *Microsoft Secrets: How the World's Most Powerful Software Company Created Technology, Shapes Markets, and Manages People.* New York: The Free Press, 1995. An interesting peek into what the most successful software firm does on a day-by-day basis.

229

Davis, Alan M. *201 Principles of Software Development.* New York: McGraw-Hill, Inc., 1995. Worth every second that you spend reading it. Although this book is for a mainframe or corporate developer, it contains gems that should be implemented for mass market software development.

Dvorak, John. *Dvorak Predicts: An Insider's Look at the Computer Industry.* Berkeley, California: Osborne McGraw-Hill, 1994. This book is an excellent barometer on the ability of the best and brightest and well connected to predict the future in this industry.

Gates, Bill. *The Road Ahead.* New York: Penguin Books USA Inc., 1995. A combination of corporate apology and vision of where the Internet is going.

Grove, Andrew S. *Only the Paranoid Survive.* New York: Currency, Doubleday, 1996. As Gates has *The Road Ahead,* Grove has *Only the Paranoid Survive.* This apology is a fascinating insight into how Intel is operated on a day-by-day basis.

Hammer, Michael and James Champy. *Reengineering the Corporation.* New York: HarperCollins Publishers, Inc., 1993. So many books bear the term *reengineering* that reading one of the first of the genre is a necessary part of modern business education.

Heckel, Paul. *The Elements of Friendly Software Design.* San Francisco, California: SYBEX Inc., 1991. This book by the inventor of "Zoom Racks" is an excellent primer on the design of computer software.

Hudgik, Steven C. *Make Money Selling Your Shareware.* New York: McGraw-Hill, Inc., 1994. No one knows more about shareware than Steve Hudgik. For those interested in pursuing shareware (and everyone should be), you can learn more about shareware from this book than any other.

Juliussen, Egil. *The Computer Industry Almanac.* Austin, Texas, annually. Need to know how many computers are in use in Africa? Or are you looking for the names of publishing directors at different companies? This book contains a huge amount of vital statistical and analytical data together with a comprehensive phone book for the computer industry.

Karrass, Chester L. *The Negotiating Game.* New York: HarperCollins Publishers, Inc., 1994. Another significant work on negotiation.

Lawler, Edward. *Underdog Marketing: Successful Strategies for Outmarketing the Leader.* New York: MasterMedia Limited, 1995. Since most of the software developers reading this book will be "underdogs," there are many creative lessons to be learned in this book.

Leebaert, Derek, ed. *The Future of Software.* Cambridge, Massachusetts: The MIT Press, 1995. An anthology with excellent thinking on the future of software development.

Mackay, Harvey. *Swim with the Sharks.* New York: Ballantine Books, 1988. A "school of hard knocks" look at entrepreneurship.

Maynard, Jr., Herman and Susan E. Mehrtens. *The Fourth Wave: Business in the 21st Century.* San Francisco: Berrett-Koehler Publishers, 1993. Books on the future are important reading for software entrepreneurs since technology has a tremendous effect on software design and development. Learning about business and leisure trends is equally as improtant. This book covers both.

McCarthy, Jim. *Dynamics of Software Development.* Redmond, Washington: Microsoft Press, 1995. One of the chief "coaches" at Microsoft shares interesting views on managing software projects and the people who make the software.

Microsoft Corporation. *The Windows® Interface Guidelines for Software Design.* Redmond, Washington: Microsoft Press, 1995. Making software follow standards is an excellent way to produce "quality" software. This is the bible for the field.

————. *Microsoft Manual of Style for Technical Publications.* Redmond, Washington: Microsoft Press, 1995. A required book to learn excellent standards for manual writing.

Negroponte, Nicholas. *Being Digital.* New York: Random House, Inc., 1995. Every software entrepreneur must read this book to understand the difference between bits and atoms. And more important, why the distinction between bits and atoms is of importance.

Popcorn, Faith. *The Popcorn Report: Faith Popcorn on the Future of Your Company, Your World, Your Life.* New York: HarperCollins Publishers, Inc., 1992. Considered to be a classic book on the near future.

Porterfield, Richard. *The Insider's Guide to Winning Government Contracts.* New York: John Wiley & Sons, Inc., 1993. This publication does not cover USPs but is an excellent grounding in the reality of government contracting.

Reis, Al and Jack Trout. *Bottom Up Marketing.* New York: McGraw-Hill, Inc., 1990. Reis and Trout offer excellent and perceptive insight into marketing. All of their books are well worth reading again and again.

————. *Marketing Warfare.* New York: Penguin Books USA Inc., 1986.

————. *Positioning: The Battle for Your Mind.* New York: McGraw-Hill, Inc., 1986.

————. *The 22 Immutable Laws of Marketing: Violate Them at Your Own Risk!* New York: HarperCollins Publishers, Inc., 1993.

Rosenberg, Rob. *Shareware: "Try Before You Buy" Software.* Las Vegas, Nevada: Paradise Publishing, 1990. The best explanation of the shareware philosophy.

Sabbagh, Karl. *Twenty-First-Century Jet.* New York: Scribner, 1996. If you want to implement the best team base management style, and truly work with suppliers as partners, this book is a must, together with the videotapes that accompany the PBS series based on the book.

Schenot, Bob. *How to Sell Your Software.* New York: John Wiley & Sons, Inc., 1994. Schenot, an expert at shareware marketing, has prepared a very good guide to creating a company that makes a living for an author. The book focuses on smaller markets rather than mass markets.

Vance, Sandra S. and Roy V. Scott. *Wal-Mart: A History of Sam Walton's Retail Phenomenon.* New York: Macmillan Publishing Company, 1994. Understanding the milieu in which one of the greatest retailing empires ever has been built is important for those who want to sell at retail.

Wallace, James and Jim Erickson. *Hard Drive: Bill Gates and the Making of the Microsoft Empire.* New York: HarperCollins Publishers, Inc., 1992. Another interesting view on how Microsoft was built.

Walton, Mary. *The Deming Management Method.* New York: The Putnam Publishing Group, 1986. An explanation of Deming's work, with particular emphasis on the psychological changes necessary for management to implement Deming-style management.

Winninger, Thomas. *Price Wars.* Rocklin, California: Prima Publishing, 1995. For those who want to try to sell at higher price points, this book on retail responses to mass discounting has interesting truths for software publishers.

One magazine and newspaper deserve special mention for software entrepreneurs.

Computer Retail Weekly. This magazine contains more intelligence on software retailing than any other single source. Also available on CMP's tech web.

The Wall Street Journal. Chunks and nuggets can be found every day in this publication.

▷ Index

Website

Please visit the web site supporting this book at: www.millionseller.com

Our website includes "dated" material including suppliers, industry contacts and up to the minute news. On a regular basis I'll also post commentaries on the latest trends, fads, and industry changes.

You can also send e-mail to me and submit contest entries. I welcome questions, comments, suggestions, and even diatribe.

The "Your Big Break" Contest

Everyone can use a "big break." And now that I've shown you how to turn your software into a million-copy seller, I'd like to throw in a bonus — I'll give the "big break" you've been looking for by offering a software publishing contract to the author of the program that I judge to have the most commercial potential.

Please note: There is no charge or obligation incurred for entering this contest. While Adams Media Corporation, the publisher of this book, has agreed to let me announce this contest here, it is solely provided by me and is not offered, administered, or endorsed by, or otherwise affiliated with, Adams Media Corporation.

The Rules
1. Entrants must submit a 500 word written abstract of their program to me at:
   herb344@aol.com (preferred) or to
   703 Pier Avenue B330, Hermosa Beach CA 90254
2. Do not send actual programs, manuals or other forms of computer media. For those submitting their abstract via mail, please enclose two business-sized stamped self-addressed return envelopes.
3. At the time of entry, the program must not already be published, except as self-published shareware.
4. The program described in the abstract must be complete, or sufficiently complete at the time of entry that it can be completed before the end of the contest.
5. All entries will be acknowledged by either return e-mail or post. At the conclusion of the contest all entrants will receive notification of the name of the winner and details of the publishing arrangement.
6. As in the real world, all entries will be reviewed, solely on the basis of the abstract, and those showing promise will be asked to submit additional materials.
7. Entrants MUST NOT contact the author directly (aside from the original entry). Any entrant making any other attempt to contact me will be disqualified from the contest.

8. Entrants may withdraw their entries at any time. They MUST withdraw their submissions if they enter into any publishing agreement (except for, as above, self-publication as shareware).

9. Entrants who have been chosen as finalists will be notified, and provided with a copy of a letter of intent setting forth all of the terms of the publishing contract — including the grant of the exclusive right to publish the title if the program is selected as the winner of the contest — on or before July 1, 1998. These letters must be executed and returned by the date specified in the notice. Contestants who decline to accept the terms of the letter of intent will not receive further consideration.

10. If for any reason the contest winner or winners do not enter into publishing contracts, the publishing contract will be awarded to the next best entry.

11. The author's decision is FINAL.

Details on how to enter the contest are also available at our Web site: www.millionseller.com.

HERBERT R. KRAFT designed *The Home and Business Legal Guide and Forms Generator*, later retitled *The PC Law Library*, which has sold nearly a million and a half copies. Between 1989 and 1992 he cohosted two nationally syndicated radio shows covering the computer business. A practicing attorney, he acts as a legal and marketing consultant for numerous computer-related clients, and is publisher for Cosmi Software — one of the leading providers of inexpensive software for consumers.